MIND OVER
MONEY

How to Live like a Millionaire
on ANY Budget

TIMOLIN R. LANGIN

WESTBOW
PRESS®
A DIVISION OF THOMAS NELSON
& ZONDERVAN

Scripture quotations taken from the Holy Bible, New Living Translation, copyright 1996, 2004. Used by permission of Tyndale House Publishers, Inc., Wheaton, Illinois 60189. All rights reserved.

Scriptures taken from the Holy Bible, New International Version®, NIV®. Copyright © 1973, 1978, 1984, 2011 by Biblica, Inc.™ Used by permission of Zondervan. All rights reserved worldwide. www.zondervan.com The "NIV" and "New International Version" are trademarks registered in the United States Patent and Trademark Office by Biblica, Inc.™ All rights reserved.

Scripture quotations are from The Holy Bible, English Standard Version® (ESV®), copyright © 2001 by Crossway, a publishing ministry of Good News Publishers. Used by permission. All rights reserved.

WestBow Press books may be ordered through booksellers or by contacting:

WestBow Press
A Division of Thomas Nelson & Zondervan
1663 Liberty Drive
Bloomington, IN 47403
www.westbowpress.com
1 (866) 928-1240

Because of the dynamic nature of the Internet, any web addresses or links contained in this book may have changed since publication and may no longer be valid. The views expressed in this work are solely those of the author and do not necessarily reflect the views of the publisher, and the publisher hereby disclaims any responsibility for them.

Any people depicted in stock imagery provided by Thinkstock are models, and such images are being used for illustrative purposes only.
Certain stock imagery © Thinkstock.

ISBN:978-1-5127-4677-8 (sc)
ISBN: 978-1-5127-4678-5 (hc)
ISBN: 978-1-5127-4676-1 (e)

Library of Congress Control Number: 2016914276

Print information available on the last page.

WestBow Press rev. date: 08/26/2016

FOREWORD

This is my granddaughter and in her I am well pleased. I am so proud of you and your achievements. I have watched you labor over this book, to make sure every word is helpful, meaningful, impactful, and life changing to every reader. You have always lived a life of excellence and integrity, even when no one was watching and through some very difficult times. Congratulations on the completion of this book. May every reader be inwardly and outwardly blessed, wealthier just for the reading.

Big Mama

DEDICATION

I would like to dedicate this book to my Big Mama who has been the most loving and influential person in my life. It is because of my praying grandmother I am who I am and have achieved what I've achieved. I have been blessed with some amazing friends who have comforted and cheered me in my time of need and celebration: Vera Jones, Lisa Pereira, Madelaine King, Dorothy "the Organizer" Breininger, Anita Whitaker, Maravillas Salazar, Sherie Blakely, Virginia Crane, Ajae Sterling, Mama... I am grateful to my God, my church, and small group for all your prayers. Ken Braskamp, Ann Blanchard, and Sarah Blanchard, you have been supportive in ways I could have never imagined. Shout out to Ann's son, Reiss, Virginia, and all who have endorsed and contributed to this book. I also dedicate this book to the many people I've met along the way via my travels at home and abroad. Thank you all for your deposits of "a little oil" (friendship) that has inspired and contributed to my life's journey resulting in this book.

ENDORSEMENTS

I couldn't put this book down! I highly recommend this financial guide to anyone who is looking for simple, practical things one can do now to decrease emotional overspending, get out of debt, make more money, and leave a legacy. Timolin strategically and wonderfully weaves a little history, a little aligning of feelings, thoughts, and actions for all of us, regardless of current financial status to live a wealthier, happier, and increasingly fun and spiritual life, all in about 100+ pages in an unconventional, but refreshingly innovative way. A must read for all who want to live like a Millionaire now!

Ann Blanchard, Agent
Creative Artist Agency

Being debt free and living rich on a modest budget is made easy in this resource. Timolin gets to the heart of our desires and teaches us to break the chains of old patterns and ingrained habits that have kept us trapped in poverty. A must read for anyone looking for prosperity: financially, mentally, and spiritually.

Victoria Fisher Briggs, Theatrical Management
Kjar & Associates

"Mind over Money" opened my eyes to the fact that not only are we emotional spenders, but in most cases we are emotional over-spenders. After reading, I feel like I went through a much needed financial rehab. No matter where you fall on the financial wealth spectrum, this is a must read and a book to refer to throughout one's lifetime.

Sara Connally
Vice-President, Creative Partnerships
and Content Universal Music Group
Vice-President, Advertising Creative
Def Jam, Island & Republic Records

An old saying, "What ye believe, that's what ye will achieve." This truism is explained succinctly in this book; therefore, every teenager to senior citizen should read this book. The principles and suggestions to a more abundant life are easy to understand and are very applicable to all. You will want to keep it near so that you can refer to it often.

Kenneth L. Braskamp
Retired, Major Wall Street Firm's
Institutional Fixed Income Division

AWESOMESAUCE!!! This is not just a book. It is a step-by-step guide, a financial coach in the palm of our hands to teach us how to save, avoid emotional overspending and most importantly create an abundant lifestyle on any budget. I am diving into each page that is so rich with information and will recommend it to all of my coaching clients. To your success with ease and grace.

Deborah Deras of Deborah Deras.com
Speaker, Author, Business Coach

Whahooooooooooo! So happy that your book has come together so beautifully! Timolin teaches that money is a tool in your life, not a tonic or tranquilizer. Her personal experience coupled with her professional insights will help design that money tool to build your dream life. Don't wait! Start now!

Dorothy "The Organizer" Breninger
Expert Organizer, A & E Hoarders TV Show

If you want to take control of your finances and enrich your lifestyle, you're going to LOVE this book! Timolin shares paradigm shifting insights that will set you free financially, and allow you to live (and feel) like a millionaire, regardless of how much money you make.

Nicole Jansen
Founder of Discover the Edge & the
Leaders of Transformation Podcast

CONTENTS

INTRODUCTORY REMARKS viii

CHAPTER 1   HOW EMOTIONAL OVERSPENDING
            IMPACTS FINANCIAL HEALTH 1

CHAPTER 2   ABOUT YOU: PROBLEM IS NOT
            JUST ABOUT YOU.................................... 8

CHAPTER 3   PARADIGM SHIFTS: FROM LESS TO BEST 13

CHAPTER 4   THE EMOTIONAL PULL ON YOUR MONEY 28

CHAPTER 5   MONEY THROUGH THE AGES 38

CHAPTER 6   TWELVE GATES INTO THE CITY
            OF PROSPERITY. HALLELU............................. 55

CHAPTER 7   SEVEN STEPS OF REAL FINANCIAL
            TRANSFORMATION...................................... 82

CHAPTER 8   WEALTH GENERATING GIFTS &
            TALENTS STEP...................................... 99

CLOSING REMARKS... 104

ABOUT THE AUTHOR.. 107

DISCLAIMER.. 109

BIBLIOGRAPHY.. 110

REFERENCES 111

INDEX... 113

INTRODUCTORY REMARKS

Do you feel like you are drowning financially? Are you looking for someone to throw you a lifeline? I am Timolin Langin and with this book I would like to extend a helping hand. I will share with you the keys to my own experience of financial stability and successful investment that allows me to live like a millionaire on a modest teacher's salary. Step by step, in the following resource I hope to show you how to begin to think and behave in new ways that over time, with focus, passion and persistence, will help you build true financial well-being, personal authenticity and strategic mastery of your money tool for the rest of your life.

Perhaps at the moment, you aren't really sure whether you need rescue, yet you do have the feeling that you are neither managing your income as effectively as you would like nor building a future as financially secure as you wish; you feel you are drifting from month to month, year to year, without purpose or direction. It seems your paycheck is gone before it arrives. Perhaps you know something is wrong in your life because debt keeps rising, income keeps falling, and financial stress keeps escalating, but you can't identify beliefs and behaviors which might be at the root of these problems. This resource is designed with you in mind.

Not long after graduating from college and starting my work life, I felt overwhelmed by a sense that I had no clue what steps to actually take to achieve what I wanted or needed financially, but I never forgot the wisdom I had gained from my great grandmother Biggie as told to me by my grandmother, whom I lovingly refer to as Big Mama. I observed the behaviors of other family members and friends who were getting themselves into financial troubles. Over time, I discovered that for many of us **money chaos and stress have emotional roots**. I began with observing their behavior and went on to discover the emotional dynamic of my own relationship to money. Still, with few resources and no outside financial help, I found a way to plan, to build and live my own life of true abundance. I write this book because I believe you will see yourself in my story.

Like me when I started my professional life, you may be looking for a mentor who knows what it is like to struggle to become financially stable, to need support and guidance along the way. I hope you may use my example and the wisdom I have gained along the way to transform your financial life from what may now be a sense of surviving from day to day to a sense of expansive happiness where you are thriving even as you desire more. As my title suggests, I intend to show you how to take your mind, money and use them to live like a millionaire. The actual amount of money needed for financial success varies; however the formula for increasing wealth and good financial stewardship is quite similar at every economic level. To get us started, I have devised a quick self-assessment inventory which may help identify some behaviors you might be employing in your relationship to the money you earn.

Simply check yes or no to each of the following ten questions.

Your Financial State of Mind

1. Do you often go shopping without a list or a goal? Yes_____ No_____
2. Does it seem that buying something lifts you out of a bad mood, at least for a while? Yes_____ No_____
3. Do you sometimes feel you need to buy something just because someone else has it? Yes_____ No_____
4. Have you ever purchased something knowing that you didn't actually have the money to pay for it, already planning to return it the next day? Yes_____ No_____
5. Are many of your purchases things you want rather than things you need? Yes_____ No_____
6. Does making a purchase make you feel a bit more alive or a bit more powerful? Yes_____ No_____
7. When you know you don't have the money in your bank account, do you rely on a credit card to get what you want right now? Yes_____ No_____

8. Do you feel that purchasing brand name products and high ticket items gives you more self-esteem or more social status? Yes _____ No _____

9. Do you spend more than you can afford on entertainment or gifts for friends and family? Yes_____ No_____

10. Have you experienced feelings of regret or shame after you make purchases for yourself or others? Yes_____ No_____
    Total: Yes _____ **No**_____

Answering "Yes" to four or more of the questions above may suggest that some of the financial distress in your life have emotional roots. Unconscious and emotional impulses to spend may be undermining your best intentions to live within or better yet below your means. Years ago, I discovered that was certainly the case for some of my friends and relatives and me. Although we did not realize it, our emotions were managing our money. I saw my friend Susan dash off to the mall every day after work. She would shop, shop, shop. Why? It seemed she was "letting off steam." Her day's frustrations, her desire to impress, her emotional need, or anger with her boyfriend would send her straight to the department store to break out her credit card and take home bags full of clothes and shoes she didn't really need, want, or wear.

I came to realize slowly that I too was giving or spending in response to emotional triggers like loneliness, wanting to belong, feeling disconnected, and periodic peer pressure. For me it seemed much of my emotional overspending was based on deep desires to feel loved by and connected to friends and family. I overspent by giving gifts and loans to others to the detriment of my own financial peace. I slowly came to realize that there were days when I too was spending in response to an emotional "trigger" like fear, sadness, boredom, doubt, or disconnection. I felt that paying a family member's rent, loaning money to pay a friend's utility bill or get my cousin's car out of impound would somehow reward me with more love and appreciation, improper thinking straightened out by co-dependency counselor, author, and colleague Stephanie Tucker.

The result of spending was the same for both Susan and me--separation from our money. In short, in my early thirties I finally was able to diagnose a growing hole in my heart based on feeling emotional lack in myself. I could see that I was self-medicating that feeling with giving away my dollars. Like some of my friends who were shopping too much, I was giving too much. We were all behaving like what I now call "emotional over-spenders." Emotional overspending is when our feelings act as spending partners, powerfully overriding our common financial sense. With our dollars we try to soothe any pain or discomfort around what is missing or lacking in our life. I do not drink, but I have come to see similarities between people who spend impulsively and alcoholics who drink compulsively. Most emotional over-spenders crave more and more, and the behavior can easily become just as compulsive and just as destructive to our present and future financial, spiritual, and emotional health as alcoholism. If your "yes" answers suggest you may be an emotional over-spender, please don't be alarmed. To varying degrees, and on occasion, we are all emotional over-spenders since emotions underlie everything we do.

However, for me, giving to soothe my emotional distress could have resulted in serious and dire financial distress if allowed to continue. So can excessive shopping. I hope that sharing my observations, experiences and self-correcting financial practices help you see triggers that set off excessive, emotional overspending behaviors in your life. You will learn new ways to identify and better respond to your own feelings and their connections to your use of your money. I have had the good fortune of having many valuable "mentally adopted" mentors in my life. Writers like Lysa Terkeurst and others I will introduce in this book have played a role in shaping my financial education about inappropriate spending and giving and the money chaos that may result. New York Times best-selling author of more than a dozen books, Terkeurst assures us that "Having issues isn't the absence of victory in our lives. It might be the very call to action needed to get you started to victory."

Recognizing a pattern of emotional overspending in your life can be a "call to action" and your most important step toward financial well-being. In my own education about money management, to my surprise, I have found that most of the books I have read about wealth building only ask you to look at and modify your current financial actions. The majority of those I have seen make little or no connection between your emotions and your money. But I believe that for us connection between what you feel and what you have or what you feel and what you do not have, must be our starting place. Seeing the connections between your feelings and the expressions of money in your life is the very first step on your path to a life of greater and lasting abundance.

I also believe that feelings of lack: lack of appreciation, lack of love, lack of hope, lack of resources, often manifest in our lives as actual lack of money. What one feels becomes what one thinks. What one thinks becomes what one does. What one does becomes what one lives. One of my favorite Bible stories is the story of "a little oil." To me it underscores the central theme of this book, ridding ourselves of lack by turning a little into a lot. This story is about a widow struggling with a profound experience of "lack" in her life. In 2 Kings 4, 1-7, we are told of a distraught woman who has lost her husband, lost her income and is about to lose her sons as well. Her sons are about to be taken away to debtor's prison because of a family debt she cannot pay.

She sought help of a spiritual leader called Elisha. The wise man asked her a key question that I am also asking you. Elisha asks the widow: "What do you have in your house?" She replies she has "nothing… but a jar of oil." She does not have "nothing" in truth. She has a little oil. This book is going to help you shift away from thinking you have nothing. See you too have a little oil, and having "a little oil" is the beginning of your rock solid financial foundation. In fact, the widow discovered it was more than enough. She found the <u>proper vessels</u> and was able to take this little oil and multiply it into more than enough money to save her sons' freedom and provide for them all for the rest of their lives. This story reveals the power of just a little oil. Like the widow, your little oil could make you wealthy when you use it <u>purposely</u>, use it <u>effectively,</u> and use it <u>strategically</u>.

However, to begin living our destined life of abundance we must align our feelings with our thoughts first so we can then align our thoughts with actions that lead to total prosperity, what I call living "like a millionaire." Sometimes we need someone like Elisha to show us the way--a mentor to help us achieve our financial and life goals. No matter what our circumstances, all we need to start our financial transformation is "a little oil." Multiply that little bit of oil with the proper attitude, take strategic actions and success will follow as it did for the widow. But what is the proper attitude toward money in our life that will reap the kind of rewards of which we dream? I believe the attitude required for living in abundance is an attitude of drive, strategic planning and generously giving back to life with what we have been blessed.

Another Bible story about a second widow's offering illustrates the importance of attitude toward what you have. She goes to the temple where it was customary for both the rich and poor to congregate and leave an offering. Jesus observes that rich men donated large sums, while the impoverished widow donated only two small coppers, yet hers was the greatest of the gifts given because she had given her all. She did not give from a place of lack but from a place of gratitude and grace. The poor widow gave the equivalent of "a ½ penny". Yet Jesus praises her gift above all, though at first glance it seems many, including the rich gave so much more. This story signifies that millions of dollars alone are not the only sign of true wealth. For me how many dollars one has in the bank is not the truest measure of abundance in one's life. Sometimes just "a ½ penny" can be the gift that transforms your life, increases fulfillment and your financial success. I hope to show you that even if you now have only a few cents or "a little oil", you can grow emotionally, financially, mentally, and spiritually into a life of total abundance, more than enough to sustain you and your family for generations.

I choose to start our generational wealth building process with focus on emotional and thinking connections to the money in your life. Once you are more aware of these connections and you have joined and strengthened some of these connections with what I call "paradigm shifts," we can clarify and boost some of our thinking about money in our lives. Then we can move on to our construction work where we start building sound and rather simple money management strategies which over time will lead you to transform financial distress into financial stability and a consistent pattern of wealth building. Why take the time to read this book? Because I want you to learn from my experience that it is possible "to live like a millionaire" even if, like me, you are a pretty ordinary, hard-working person, even an underdog.

Becoming aware of emotional overspending and its triggers is essential to overcoming financial debt and feelings of lack and to increase and maintain unending wealth. For that reason we will focus first on decreasing emotional spending, exercising clear thinking, managing triggers, and staying motivated to build our own wealth over time. Family influences and dynamics are also included; as home is where many of our initial ideas about money matters and money management are formed and indirectly taught. In Chapter Two, we focus on becoming more aware of connections between feelings and money by highlighting what I call "paradigm shifts." In Chapters Three and Four we focus specifically on changes needed in our thinking about our relationship to money. In Chapters Five – Eight we initiate the actions needed for financial wealth building with seven sound and rather simple money management strategies which begin the transformation from financial stress into financial success and prepare the soil for the seeds of a rich harvest of wealth in your life. This financial guide closes with a discussion about Legacy and provide more insight about the author. No matter what your financial circumstances right now, I believe this book will show you how to use "mind over money" to "live like a millionaire" on YOUR budget.

CHAPTER 1

HOW EMOTIONAL OVERSPENDING IMPACTS FINANCIAL HEALTH

If your answers to the earlier ten question quiz on Financial State of Mind indicated there may be a pattern of emotional overspending in your life at this moment, then it's time you begin to turn around your financial life. Identifying and limiting emotional overspending is the foundation of building the wealth you want. I found that growing my awareness of my emotional "triggers" and connecting my emotional "state of mind" to its expression in my spending behaviors was the beginning of my personal transformation to the increasingly abundant life I have built for myself.

I have had the good fortune of having parents, a grandmother and a great grandmother who modeled thoughtful money management, attention to fiscal details; demonstrated powerfully in their lives how a small, but well-managed income could yield a life of abundance. My formative years of foundation building mirror their money lives. Like my family and the woman with "a little oil," I started with few resources. After college, I lived in a 400 square feet apartment paid for by my low level job paying $8.00 an hour in South Central Los Angeles. I will show you how I took that "little oil" and turned it into a beautiful lifestyle of multiple properties, exotic vacations, and new business interests.

My family's examples were my most important asset at the time, and in truth they still are. My powerful and kind grandmother, in particular, taught me honesty, responsibility and conscious daily care of my income, no matter how small it was. She taught me, as well, to raise my eyes to envision a future radiant with promise, passion and prosperity. With my small income, honorable work and humble apartment, I focused on staying in the black financially and kept driving ahead. Around me, at this same time however, I could see many of my peers falling into money traps of all sorts: huge student loans, multiple credit cards, impulse purchases, apartment rents which left them penniless at the end of the month. I saw these gifted people feel more and more helpless, discontent, depressed. They despaired of their low checking account balances, piles of bills, and deferred dreams.

I came to see that many of them had become what I now call "Emotional Over-spenders." They were men and women caught in patterns of spending without thinking about consequences, buying unconsciously, purchasing to soothe some painful feeling or rejoice in a transient triumph. Eager advertisers, happily help us soothe our pain, this way. I appreciate now what good fortune I had to have a legacy of money wisdom from my family. Like most of us, I didn't learn how to balance a check book or figure out my own taxes in any class at school. All my early financial training came from observing my Big Mama, who had a 9th grade education and worked as a cook in wealthy homes in Mississippi and her mother who worked as a sharecropper and had no formal education. Their reputations for financial prudence and responsibility are my inspiration, and their wit and wisdom still guide me through my own complex and busy money life today.

Though I lived in the Mississippi Delta, one of the poorest regions of the United States, I grew up middle class. As I grew up and traveled far from home to Los Angeles, I became more and more aware of the differences between the "haves" and the "have nots." When I moved as a teenager to the city of lights, camera, and action, l began to feel "less than." I went to a new high school where everyone wore designer clothes, fancy shoes, and lots of "bling." But my family's values kept me going. They taught me to value education, focused work, and money sense as paths to a good life and financial health. I still remember being about ten years old when I accompanied my grandmother, Big Mama, to a major department store in our town where she asked the Manager to extend credit on a purchase she wanted to make on behalf of her mother, Biggie. Biggie was so respected in town for her honesty and fiscal responsibility that I saw the Manager agree right then and there to her proposal with only a smile and a handshake. Try using that kind of "social credit" in a store today!

But Biggie was in clear contact with her own self-worth and brought that to bear on all her transactions with others. I appreciate now, all these years later, the inspiration I draw from Big Mama's and Biggie's powerful sense of their own great personal worth. They gave me the foundation of my understanding of how to live within my means and avoid the traps of mindless shopping and peer envy. Their type of financial clout is still available to us today. Later I will show you how I got banks to help me further my well-planned goals. Banks have loaned me money based on my word alone--no credit checks or collateral. Establishing strong personal relationships with people around you in your community, your church, and your social organizations can create knowledge, "wit" (the effective application of knowledge), and financial savvy that could lead to banking transactions similar to mine.

Like my family members, I hold tight to the belief that the most important credit I can have in this world is a good reputation and unwavering belief in my own personal worth. Do not get me wrong. I value my nice car, my beautiful clothes, and my investment properties, and I am full of gratitude that I have a net worth in dollars that my family could only dream of fifty years ago. But I remain firm in the understanding that my true worth in this world resides only in me, not in my possessions or the dollars in my bank account. My "net worth" is merely a byproduct of my awareness of my true worth. Believe me when I say I am not a financial insider. I have no degree in economics or business. I do not know a hedge fund from a hedgehog.

I do, however, have a lifetime of experiences that have worked abundantly well for me. I have never gone without anything I've wanted because I have great relationships with a variety of institutions and people, including my bank, my car dealer, my real estate agent. I have learned like the woman with "a little oil" how to generate a lot from a little and live like a millionaire on my modest teaching salary. I want to show you how you can do the same. I will share as much as I can in this book, but know that more information can be found when you visit my website or participate in my workshops about the role of your money in building your own rich life.

For almost two decades I have been a successful public school teacher. I have built my own impressive portfolio of real estate properties, enjoyed a bevy of glamorous trips to exotic destinations, and started my own communications business. I first set out to help others with financial education in my classroom, public talks, and public workshops. Now my mentoring activities, financial literacy classes, and workshops are available through the enterprise I proudly call New Fit World TV at the website www.newfitworldtv.com. With my enterprise I want to show you how to have a "new fit" or new relationship with your money. I want to extend my mentoring to the entire world through the power of the internet and the many media outlets available to us in the 21st century. Research reveals a huge need for my message since I watch so many talented people: friends, clients, and even seemingly rich, rich people battle valiantly against financial distress.

This book is a further extension of my mentoring endeavors. You may be surprised as we begin that I don't recommend deprivation as a starting place, though some initial restraint in spending will be necessary. On the contrary, I firmly believe we all need to marry more conscious spending with as much pleasure as we can introduce into our day to day lives. I ultimately want to show you how to enjoy the things you want most in life without financial strain or pain. I believe it is possible for pleasure and financial success to coexist. In other words, you can be a good steward of your money and enjoy the good life too. So, my purpose in this book is to help you see, plan and start to live a more purposeful life, a life which may become richer than you can even imagine **now**; a life that will inspire your friends as well as enrich the lives of your family members for generations. We all need purpose in our lives. Eleanor Roosevelt expressed the meaning of "purpose" as I use the term here: "The purpose of life is to live it, to taste experience to the utmost, to reach out eagerly and without fear of newer and richer experience."

However, before any seed of new purpose can grow it has to have good soil and good water and good care. For this reason, I choose to focus first on the soil of the emotional and thinking aspects of your relationship to money and then move on to productive and fruitful management practices that I have personally used to generate financial success--practices that will benefit you as a working person as well. Know that in order to change your life in ways that lead to more abundance, you will probably need to change some feelings you have now, change some thoughts you do not question, and change some behaviors with which you are very comfortable. That sounds like a lot of change, but the challenge is worth taking when we consider and seek the rewards, and experience the financial benefits of our new way of life. You do not have to take this money journey alone. Greater awareness of the underlying emotional dynamics of your own money life, connections between your personal history, your feelings, and your thoughts will give you greater hope and confidence that you too can live the life of your dreams. Then I will highlight some sound and surprisingly simple management skills you can employ to increase financial stability, increase savings, increase income, increase investing power and with time, live like a millionaire on your budget.

However, before we can go further, we've got to do some brain surgery on you. Don't be alarmed. If you see characteristics of an "Emotional Over-spender" in your answers to the quiz on Financial State of Mind, you may already be anticipating that we need to address this underlying cause of some of your money issues. I firmly believe that how you FEEL is directly connected to how you THINK and how you THINK is directly connected to how you SPEND right now, and how you SPEND is directly connected to being less wealthy than you would like in this moment in your life. Therefore, Chapter Two guides you through a process of altering "paradigms," feeling and thinking structures that currently drive your money behaviors into undesirable outcomes. In order to live the financial life of your dreams, some minor tweaking may be needed in some areas and major tweaking in others.

According to Zoe Henry, author of "5 Smart Money-Saving Tips from Tony Robbins' Financial Adviser" emotional decisions are the biggest destroyer of wealth.[1] I agree. That is why we start with emotions here. I show you how simple shifts in feelings can cause shifts in your thinking. And new thinking can lead directly to new actions which make building wealth easier for you. Emotional and mental preoccupations with consuming hinder financial progress and deny us the life we long to live. We were born to produce and live according to our passion or purpose and nothing else! We've been accepting substitutes far too long. The purpose of this book is to shed light on this connection between your inner life and your actual money. The first conversation we need to have involves identifying some emotions you may be allowing to block realization of your own money goals. Then we will explore what kind of thinking is built on those emotions and examine how that kind of thinking gets expressed as non-productive money behaviors.

Now, I do not say that these changes will be easy. I am, in many ways, still an emotional little girl inside. I have and I continue to struggle with fear, doubt, and insecurity in pursuit of my life purpose. I am still the girl who can have a hard time deciding what to do next. However, through the legacy of my great grandmother's wit and Big Mama's wisdom, I have succeeded in mustering enough clarity, courage, and direction to act in ways that have allowed me to blossom personally and financially so that today I do live in the kind of abundance that makes me happy and my existence satisfying. You can do the same right now, regardless of your income.

Wealth building and abundant living are first and foremost a state of mind. I will speak about the state of mind we may seek as we proceed. I will flow between "I and we," "yours and ours," and "you and me" to simply reinforce the idea that we are taking this journey together. You and I and other wealth builders can construct a financial community of "being" where we come together to encourage each other, share wealth building tips, celebrate financial achievements, and know that we are not alone in our life journey. The miracle of the internet makes it so much easier for us to both learn and connect these days. This kind of financial information, guidance, and connection was just not as available and accessible when I was building my financial foundation years ago. So take advantage of these new and nearly infinite resources as much as you can. Use this book and visit website, www.newfitworldtv.com, to gather additional resources, links, and practical tips to guide you on your financial journey. Establish connections with me and with others who wish to build their lives in new ways: ask your questions, post your own advice, record your own progress, take money challenges, and review and guide your thinking and actions as we proceed together.

In truth, we can create our own powerful "network" by sharing what we learn. Tell us about a good sale going on in Chicago or a special restaurant to visit in Rome or what eateries are giving away a free scoop of ice cream today, or give us the name of the best credit union's interest rates in your state. Pooling our knowledge and our resources help us increase our financial power, stay committed to our goals, and increase our wealth by simply spending our money strategically and effectively. This book is not just a book on how to get out of debt. This is a book about how to get rid of the **debt weight** once and for all, and throw off other emotional and spiritual weights that hold us down and keep us from flourishing and having fun, the "time of our life."

On how many occasions have we gotten excited about something then fizzled out quickly? Think about those annual "New Year" resolutions to lose weight and just a few weeks in, we think it's too hard and we revert to our old habits. Now you see the reason for the network. Having partners as well as a global support network readily available makes the journey easier, more significant, and more fun. So let us partner on this life journey of losing **"financial weight"** and **create new habits** by sharing tips, strategies, stories, and great places to visit and shop, find accommodations, etc., all over the world at affordable or discount prices.

REFLECTION: Have you ever made a New Year's Resolution to become financially fit? Explain what worked well and what did not work so well.

CHAPTER 2

ABOUT YOU: PROBLEM IS NOT JUST ABOUT YOU.

The quality of one's life is determined by the decisions one makes, and perhaps, sometimes even by how one feels. Timolin

Lottery Jackpot 100 million, 200 million, 300 million dollars! Power Ball-- a billion dollar jackpot! Get your ticket now! I know colleagues who pooled their dollars to buy Lotto tickets and strike it rich. Like them, we've all asked at one point what would we do if we hit the lotto or magically come into a large sum of money. I have done the same. I ask this question in my workshops all the time and here are some of the most common answers for those money imaginations, in no particular order:

- Buy a New Car
- Buy a House
- Take a Dream Vacation
- Pay Off Credit Card Debt
- Start a Business
- Go to College
- Quit Work

Like my Workshop attendees, we all daydream and wonder how our life would change if a large windfall fell into our laps. You're probably imagining all the things you could do. How about doing these things right now? You can have all of these common money dreams come true right now, with the exception of quitting your job. Perhaps you smile and chuckle. But it's true! What I say to my workshop attendees is the same thing I will say to you and that is "You can have those dreams come true in your life with your current income." What does it take on your part? No, not buying a lottery ticket! Rather, I am going to ask you to start FEELING and THINKING differently than you are accustomed to right now. With some adjustments to your perception of wealth and abundance, you can recreate yourself as a wealthier, healthier, and happier person. Keep your job because you will need it to grow your wealth, at least to start with, unless you are expecting a big inheritance in the near future or that lottery win.

Find the millionaire inside you—inside your feelings, your ideas, beliefs, and later greater abundance can manifest through your proper actions. To successfully change our money lives requires change around both feeling and thinking. It requires a willingness to try something unfamiliar. I am reminded of a Facebook post which says… "If you have already been trying hard, maybe trying harder is not the way. Try different." That axiom is really true. Doing more of what doesn't work while expecting a different outcome is the very definition of "stuck." If you go on doing what you are doing now, you will get the same unhappy result. That's why success in our endeavor requires **a shift in feelings and thoughts, and then new actions can follow and new paths can open.**

What do I mean by suggesting that we need to begin our work with a "SHIFT" in feelings and thoughts? You know that to "SHIFT" means to change. However, I am suggesting that you do not merely change your feeling and thinking. I want you to transform your own feeling and thinking about both money and life. In fact, I am going to suggest how radical a change I am asking you to make by using the phrase "PARADIGM SHIFT." I am stealing this term from Thomas Kuhn's well known 1960's work on philosophy and history of science, <u>The Structure of Scientific Revolutions</u>. Paradigm refers to a pattern of belief systems, values, and thought that may or may not be true, in fact a paradigm may not even be conscious.

Yet, our paradigm constructs shape our behaviors and have a huge impact on how we live life, oftentimes determining the very quality of our lives. According to Kuhn, scientific knowledge has moved forward not in a smooth line but in great lurches created by occasional radical rethinking of our views of the world, a rethinking often instigated by one astute and brave observer. What we are doing in Part One of this book is urging a series of "PARADIGM SHIFTS" in your feeling and thinking that may overturn or renew your views and, as a result, change your behaviors in your financial life to increase financial success. You may remember learning in school about an example of a major "paradigm shift" in science created in the 1400s by the Renaissance astronomer Copernicus from his own simple, solitary, clear eyed observations of the ways planets actually moved as he studied them carefully with his telescope. For a thousand years before, most humans, those in European cultures anyway, were firmly convinced that the sun and all other planets moved in great gracious cycles around the earth, making human life and its earthly home the center of the universe, as they saw it.

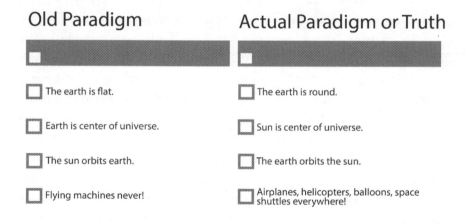

Old Paradigm	Actual Paradigm or Truth
☐ The earth is flat.	☐ The earth is round.
☐ Earth is center of universe.	☐ Sun is center of universe.
☐ The sun orbits earth.	☐ The earth orbits the sun.
☐ Flying machines never!	☐ Airplanes, helicopters, balloons, space shuttles everywhere!

I am not a scientist or financial spiritualist who proposes to overwhelm you with talk about science and the psyche. But I am absolutely certain that there are some scientific approaches we can take to increase wealth in all areas leading to a new financial life that can only arise from a new way of viewing the nature of money and your relationship to it. Whether one knows it or not, one is always acting out of various conscious or unconscious feeling or belief paradigms. That is, one's actions arise from patterns of feeling and thoughts that may have always been unexamined and unquestioned. These patterns are often conventions or assumptions we absorb or accept as the "givens" of our lives. The loss of a paradigm is not a bad thing, but it is sure to be a transformation in some way.

Think about hearing Christopher Columbus talk of his trip around the world. Then look at the faces around you when you declare the world is flat, still. Think about American history in just the last century or so. Compare the world of your grandparents with yours. They may have been absolutely sure that a human being was never going to fly. You know that today for a few dollars you can fly anywhere in the world in a few hours. Your grandfather may have believed that women and minorities should never own property or vote for government representatives. Then along came powerful views of people like Susan B. Anthony and Martin Luther King, Jr. As a result, today you and I see our society quite differently than those in your grandparents' generation. We've come a long way, baby!

You have unconsciously internalized very different, radically new, paradigms of technology and social structure than they had. However, you may be surprised to learn that in the twenty first century you may still be operating out of the same or very similar paradigms that they used for their relationship to money in the nineteenth century. So when research tells us that 90% of our everyday behaviors, even our most important behaviors like spending, are controlled by our unconscious mind, it is prudent to stop and examine and raise to conscious scrutiny our feelings and belief patterns, our money paradigms. Are our financial lives operating like we believe the earth is flat or that the sun revolves around our little planet? If you identified with "yes" answers to the questions in the "Financial State of Mind" Quiz, then you may be operating in your life as an "Emotional Over-spender." Great, because you cannot fix something which is outside of your awareness. The quiz itself may be enough to help you recognize some ways in which you are mis-connecting feelings with spending money. You may now see some of your seemingly innocent behaviors as active self-sabotage.

When you are overtired, you treat yourself to an expensive restaurant dinner as a reward for working so hard, even though you can't afford it. When you feel angry, you soothe your ruffled feathers with a day at the spa or an expensive gym membership. When you feel desirous of your friend's new car or your cousin's new house, you may attempt to "keep up with the Joneses" by keeping that shiny gold credit card very busy. You start to feel uneasy, uncomfortable with the emotions underneath your spending. Although these uncomfortable feelings may never go away permanently, they can be contained and certainly acted upon less when aware. In fact, the day after is likely to lead to more feelings: feelings of remorse, sadness, and a need to spend more and more. And the resulting debt created by these attempts to "fix" one's emotional discomfort in the world is likely to become your own very real and seemingly permanent financial disaster. You are truly not conscious of what you are doing in the moment.

Overspending, obviously, often results in major debt, especially if, like most of us today, you use a credit card, or a dozen credit cards, to make your purchases. A credit card seems to make the consequences of a purchase invisible. Only later, when the bills arrive, do you become aware that your expenditures exceeded your income for the month! You may be genuinely shocked to discover how much you spent. Even with a big bill in hand, you may go right back to shopping to cure your sense of emotional ills. You may go on spending, knowing you do not have the funds, because a purchase, a purchase of almost anything sometimes, gives a momentary and an illusory sense of power, or a brief sense of having more personal value.

I will share some tips that have helped many be successful in quieting these feelings to limit spending/overspending to soothe emotions or ease an upset or disappointment. I believe that Emotional Overspending is the consequence of a very outdated financial paradigm which encourages your mind to misdirect your behavior. Here is where we begin our process of financial transformation of your life. I would like to introduce you in the next few pages to five familiar but outdated financial paradigms that you may be employing in your financial world view right now. We will then begin the process of transforming your feeling and thinking patterns by helping you see five new ways of understanding your relationship to the money in your life. We will look first at a belief pattern that you may be using in an unquestioning way, but the belief, this old paradigm, even if it was once true, is no longer supported by our life experiences. Then we will look at a different pattern, a new paradigm, one that has transformational and lasting consequences for your relationship to your financial life and your financial success.

CHAPTER 3

PARADIGM SHIFTS: FROM LESS TO BEST

Our goal is to "SHIFT" our feeling and thinking from each old dysfunctional pattern to a new way of feeling and thinking which will then become the basis of new ways of acting. This portion of our work in the next pages focuses on introducing "paradigm shifts" in your thinking about the role of money in your life. With each "shift," a radical new way of looking at the same concept, you may experience a change in your feelings, a change in your thinking and then a change in your behaviors that may revolutionize your relationship to the money in your life. Here is the first of the five PARADIGM SHIFTS I would like you to consider in your movement toward greater financial well-being. Here is the first conventional or traditional way of thinking about money you may have absorbed as you grew up, that may have seemed logical at the time or may have just gone unquestioned, just accepted as normal.

OLD PARADIGM: Spending money makes you feel better.

SHIFT # 1

NEW PARADIGM: Money is a tool in your life, not a tonic or a tranquilizer.

Where did that old paradigm come from? Perhaps your parents gave you spending money when you were very young in order to help you learn to "handle" finances in your life. But the problem is obvious. Often this money, this "allowance," was "given" to you with very little guidance or instruction. And it was just for "spending!" We simply spent our allowances with very little, if any discussions about spending limits, debilitating debt, or money savvy. There were few family talks about saving, strategic spending, or a look to the future. The unquestioned connection between money and childhood freedoms, self-satisfactions, and carefree comforts was made early and solidly in our youth, with no consideration of consequences or possible outcomes. But as adults earning limited incomes and having to support ourselves, we are learning we cannot afford to live with the unconscious and unquestioned childhood belief that money is just for "spending."

In a later chapter, we will stress that money is a tool in our life, a tool to be used thoughtfully and skillfully. Mindless spending is only one of many ways in which we put money to use in our lives, and it is not necessarily the best, most important or even the most pleasurable way, though it may feel that way at the time of purchase. Ironically, if you have been overspending in your life, you have actually proven to yourself quite dramatically that spending does not lead to feeling better; that more often it actually leads to feeling even worse than you did before. I have helped many overcome their overspending habits, and I assure you that you can do the same by seeing yourself and your money in radically new ways.

This old paradigm that money is just for spending is almost universal in our culture. But, as you will see, this view of the world is not only outdated, it is patently false. Your money is a tool with many other functions in your life to build and create the life you want. Have you ever thought about a **purposeful dollar**? We will explore this concept later. But first, let's look at four other very basic paradigms of money beliefs that you may have absorbed and may be employing in your life without really knowing you are doing so. Let's take a look at conventional money paradigm # 2, a belief pattern that most of us grow up accepting without question.

OLD PARADIGM: I do not have enough money.

SHIFT # 2

NEW PARADIGM: I already have enough to live well and happily.

Ask yourself "What am I worth?" You might answer by totaling up the current value of your house, your car and your bank account. If you see your worth in this way, you are likely to always feel you must have more: more dollars, more objects, more stuff. It is very common for us to feel that we do not have enough, certainly not as much as the next guy! Seeing yourself as already having enough will completely transform your existence and your peace of mind. The truth is that in Twenty First Century American and western society at large, and in most other first world or wealthy countries of our globe, if you have a gross income equivalent to $ 50,000 - $75,000 dollars, you are already richer than 90% of all the people on this planet. If you are a woman with that income level, you are richer than about 99% of all the other females on this planet. It has recently been estimated that one half of the world's population lives on about $2.50 a day, and about 80% of the world's population lives on less than $10.00 a day. Seen in this light, you are already one of the wealthiest and most privileged inhabitants of this planet. If you can become acutely aware of the reality that you already have "enough," you will have the foundation of a very rich life.

The pressure of our consumer society constantly works on us to believe that we do not have enough. We must buy more. We must own more. We must earn more. We must be more. The result of this old paradigm is a constant sense and state of living in LACK. An unconscious whisper tells you again and again that you are not enough and you do not have enough, or certainly you don't have anywhere near as much as those around you. And this small sad inner voice drives a person to suffer inwardly and seek to soothe that suffering with consuming continually. In truth, you are blessed right now no matter the amount of your income. You are enough and you have enough. You may just want more; a very clear, financially healthy, and important distinction to make. A third familiar old paradigm inherited from our social history is closely related to the second and equally harmful to one's financial well-being:

OLD PARADIGM: I must have more money in order to be happier.

SHIFT # 3

**NEW PARADIGM: The more I appreciate
what I already have, the happier I am.**

The amount of income you have, after you have enough to cover your survival needs, does not directly correlate to happiness in your life. In truth, if you are a middle class wage earner, you do not need more to be content. It is pretty well established, for example, that winning a vast sum in the lottery does not make a winner happy. In fact, many lottery winners burn through their windfalls very quickly and end up bankrupt in a relatively short time. Recent psychological research reveals you do not have to hit the Lotto or come into a large windfall to live the good life. If your income is in the aforementioned middle class dollar range, then you can be as happy as the average millionaire or even billionaire just as you are. If you believe you are already truly rich, then that thought itself will govern your behavior and will have a profound impact on what you actually achieve.

Consider a TIME magazine article titled "PSYCHOLOGY OF MONEY, Why $50,000 May Be the (New) Happiness Tipping Point" by Josh Sanburn, dated April 19, 2012. Sanburn tells us that "A new poll by the Marist Institute for Public Opinion suggests that as little as $50,000 brings genuine happiness. In every category surveyed, those earning $50,000 were more satisfied with their lot, suggesting that $50,000 is the tipping point."[2] The verdict is in and it says you do not have to have a lot of money to be happy. Happiness is an inside job. Living like a millionaire requires an adjusted state of mind rather than just an adjusted or higher dollar amount in the bank. To further cement this paradigm shift, let's take a look at another article. An article in The Guardian, "The Price of Happiness," September 6, 2010, referenced an American study that says "A survey of 1,000 Americans found that happiness rose in line with salary, but only until people earned $75,000 a year….Perhaps $75,000 is a threshold beyond which further increases in income no longer improve an individuals' ability **to do what matters most to their emotional well-being**…."[3] Happiness is not equal to dollars in your bank account.

The revolution in thinking is the fact that you and I can be as happy as the super wealthy with our current incomes once we abandon ill-serving and erroneous assumptions about the role of money in our lives and begin to use our money as a tool to build abundance more strategically and purposefully. I will even say your income can be less than $50,000 and you can still share in the same happiness. I give this analogy in my focus groups: Who is most wealthy, a person making $40,000 a year with all bills paid, sleeping well at night, and surrounded by friends and family or someone making one million dollars per year whose living expenses total two million per year and whose nights are sleepless and whose family quarrels fiercely because they too feel the pressure of lack? I know people who fall into both categories. The person with less stress has a lot more peace of mind, a larger measure of happiness; attributes that could never be defined by just dollars.

In the tiny country of Bhutan, the government has expressed a new paradigm of well-being in the notion of its Gross National Happiness Index. The leaders of this country are promoting the revolutionary idea that the measure of the well-being of the people of Bhutan is not their income but their personal contentment, their sense of social harmony and familial security. Shifting your feeling and thinking about the nature of happiness is key to a new financial state of mind and a new financial life. There is far more to abundant living than just money alone. You will soon see that having money alone can cause many problems, even for the very wealthy. I throw this in to inject humor, but I was having a conversation with a former colleague who always works as an assistant to multi-millionaires and she says we working people are endlessly trying to get more and the multi-millionaires are desperately trying not to lose what they have. Both are unhealthy ways to live. Emotions we are unaware of and belief patterns that are outdated but still operating on our behaviors without our intention lead to money struggles no matter what our incomes.

Whether your income is fifty thousand or five million dollars a year, debt, my friend, will destroy your peace of mind and **usually debt, not lack of money, is the reason a person does not feel rich**. Millionaires who have a lot of debt do not feel rich, regardless of how many things they have. The same wealthy family mentioned above constantly talks about the toll debt has taken on family life even though they've got a lot of "toys."

Non-rich families who struggle with debt and not having enough for basic necessities also experience difficulties and stress. Money challenges of life are common to us all. We think we need more money to be happy, yet I haven't found a single study that supports such a statement. I am convinced we can feel both happy and rich on our current incomes. I can say that because for years I have lived a life which is happy and in which I experience great abundance though I have the modest income of a public school teacher. I use my income as a tool to do things I love and to pursue my passion for seeing the world. I love to travel and one of my favorite music artists and friend performs frequently all over the world. I often travel to her concerts, and I sometimes joke that when I am in Paris I see the same sights Beyonce sees, though she has the benefit of celebrity and millions of dollars. I walk the same streets, admire the same Eiffel Tower, and wander the same Louvre. True, no one rolls out the red carpet when I arrive and my hotel bed may not have Egyptian cotton sheets, but I can still say I have a BALL every time I go to Paris, the beautiful City of Lights.

Why do I feel like I have it all? My growing sense of authenticity, wealth, and total well-being is created by me, by my paradigm shift; my financial well-being is not good fortune or an accident! I am not the lucky one! I had a vision in high school and took strategic, **scientific, formulaic steps** to make the dream a reality. So can you! Money is a tool. Every day we can use that tool to build the life we want as part of what I like to call a financial design for living. I am going to show you how to design plans for your income which will allow you to live the life you want NOW while working toward your ultimate goal with mastery of **your** money tool and instituting strategic and deliberate conscious management.

Don't get me wrong. Like you, I still desire more. But I don't desire more because I feel I am not enough as I am. Remember, in our new feeling and thinking paradigm we do not equate having more money or more things with being more satisfied and content. I want you to be happy with what you have at this very moment, and I want you to hold on to that new belief that you are already happy and rich as you take steps to make your life flourish even more. You may be laughing at me now, but I am determined to help you see how wealthy you already are today. Our fourth paradigm shift may be the single most powerful and transforming change in your thinking patterns.

Old Paradigm: Work harder, longer, to get wealthier.

SHIFT # 4

New Paradigm: Thinking wealthier will make you wealthier.

Do you believe that all work and no play will make Jack a rich boy eventually? We have earlier established that as working class people with a decent income, you are already rich, super rich actually. Compared to so many people in the world who live at subsistence level, you have what you need to not just survive, but thrive: food, water, housing, clothing and more, even electricity and running water, cable television and cell phone and your own automobile in all likelihood. Your life, even if you are discontent with it right now, is already blessed with uncommon comforts, even luxuries.

Some time ago, I happened to hear Mark Cuban being interviewed on the Queen Latifah Show. Cuban is a very successful entrepreneur, owner of the Dallas Mavericks and the Landmark Theaters chain. Cuban was offering the TV audience advice on money and power on the basis of his own success in building great wealth and a vast investment empire. Cuban told the talk show host and recording artist, Queen Latifah "It's not so much whether you see the cup as half empty or half full. What matters is that you are the one pouring the water." Think about being, feeling thirsty (pause) and now feel, think and know that you already have what it takes to pour yourself a cup of water. Whether the water is actually beside you, knowing that a cup is quickly accessible quenches your thirst and gives you a sense of empowerment.

With Cuban's vivid image in mind, let's take a look at how we pour water with a very modest income. My teaching income was once close to the higher end of the range, but with decreasing school budgets and downsizing, my salary, like yours and perhaps others you know, has been lowered during the budget cuts and tight times of our nation's recent financial downturn. Who can remember the last time a raise was given? Yet, in spite of the economy, I have used my money as a tool to buy multiple investment properties, travel to six continents, and pursue my vision and passion for life by opening a business intent on teaching men and women, how they too can live like millionaires on ordinary incomes, regardless of fluctuations in the economy or where you live.

Of course, a new life begins with embarking on a new way of thinking about what true wealth is and how we achieve it. I would venture to say the traditional thinking paradigms and traditional methods of "getting ahead" are not working for most of us emotional money managers. We've always been taught to work hard, get good grades, study long hours, and then and only then will we be financially rewarded. How has that way of thinking been rewarding you? Don't most of us work hard? Perhaps you not only work hard, but you also do your best to work smarter too! But you find that you are working harder and working smarter and still you are struggling, perhaps even failing.

The truth is our schools do not prepare us for our money lives. They don't tell us how to handle the money we make, how to really make money, how to balance our checkbooks, develop budgets, calculate our taxes and so on. Perhaps you had a savvy money mentor in your family as I did. If so, you are fortunate. But many people don't know how to pour their own water. My friend, Richard Vale, once said to me with great dismay, "Sometimes it seems that the harder I work the less effective I am." A true story from my life vividly demonstrates this experience of the futility of hard work alone. I recall having to take this huge credentialing exam (80 to 90% failure rate) near the end of my college years that would have an impact on my ability to earn a living. I had two options: pass it and continue to work or fail it and find myself a new career.

Pressure on! I worked hard and smart according to traditional test preparation standards. I created a study plan, carved out the right quiet location to work in and set aside numerous hours for my efforts. I spent weeks and weeks studying, while still working full-time, only to fail the exam. After failing the first time, I resorted to an expensive traditional preparatory class, studied long and hard and failed again. Surely, the third time would be the charm. So, what did I do? I continued to work even harder, put in even longer hours, secured additional study guides and still failed the exam. The third time was not the charm. All of that time, hard work and intense effort yielded no positive results. Working harder, longer, even smarter, did not yield success. Now, Timolin the emotional money magnet became more and more scared, nervous, and panicked that she might never pass the exam, never earn the right to go on working! I then truly understood the concept of diminishing returns. The more I studied, the harder I worked, the more I stressed, the lower my test scores. Like Richard, I found I was working harder and becoming less, not more, effective. If I had continued down that path, I truly believe I would have never passed that exam and I might now be working in some other career entirely, one without my lovely long summer vacations.

But, as you know, I am still a teacher. Somehow I found a way to succeed on that examination. What was the solution to my dilemma? Another exam preparation sitting that had a different and positive outcome. I experienced my own paradigm shift after enduring all those repeated disappointments. Hard work clearly did not equal success. I needed motivation to go on and a new approach to obtain a better result. For help I inwardly adopted an amazing, effective quote by Tony Robbins, life coach, motivational speaker, and writer. His words offered me a paradigm shift that helped me out of my stuck place. I had to leave behind the old paradigm that hard work and long study hours would make me successful. I had to work differently, which leads me to the next paradigm.

**Old Paradigm: Repeat what you are doing
harder and longer in order to succeed.**

SHIFT # 5

New Paradigm: Take different action to get a different result.

Robbins' point is very succinct: "If you do what you've always done, you'll get what you've always gotten." Studying for that test with traditional methods over and over, longer and harder, did not work for me, and I would venture to say the traditional methods of working and earning a living day in and day out may not be giving you the result you seek either. I was full of fear. What if I don't pass? Where would I work? How would I make a living? How would I make ends meet while looking for a new job? Did I have any skills that would qualify me for some other career? These are common kinds of worries for us, particularly those of us who operate as insecure and emotional money managers. I am giving my all and it's not working. What to do? With Robbins' words as inspiration and with additional encouragement from a colleague, I did not give up. I tried again. This time, however, I prepared in a new and unorthodox way. I heard about a unique approach to taking exams from a colleague and went to the workshop with her and I wound up passing the exam the very next time.

So what was so different or unorthodox? The workshop helped me change my feelings about the nature of the test and shifted my thinking about preparation work itself. What I remember most is how much fun the presenters and students were having in these classes. We were learning the same materials I had studied before on my own but now from a different perspective as they were taught in a method that was geared toward "passing tests" and less labor intensive i.e. less studying associated with traditional test preparation. The instructors spent less time covering the concept or items to be tested and more time covering the **mindset** of test makers, showing us how test questions are structured, and relevant answering and effective guessing strategies, that when in doubt would be accurate most of the time. In education, we call it lowering the "affective" or emotional filter. That class helped me shift my feeling about the nature of the test experience and helped me **think outside the box** about how the test was made rather than how the test was "taken." I had to adapt and adopt a new approach or way of thinking that corresponds to passing this and most exams, and learn to relax and enjoy the journey or process of the **strategic application of knowledge learned**. What can be more relaxing than repeating this phrase over and over, "It's easy, and I like it!" "It's easy, and I like it!" "It's easy, and I like it!" What do you think the outcome was the next time?

Yes, you got it right! The next time was different. As you know, I passed the exam! I didn't just pass it; I passed it with less effort, fewer hours studying and less stress. I spent more time seeing and understanding the big picture and how it related to smaller, essential components. I listened to people who had seen the test-taking task in new ways and shared this new perspective that I needed to achieve my goal. A shift in thinking and a willingness or perhaps I should say total **desperation** led to a change in my feelings and thinking about how to approach and take the exam and only then did I get my desired result. The biggest revelation of all was learning that there is a scientific approach to test taking and tapping into it made a significant and most powerful difference. All of these applications are true when it comes to prosperous money management. Prosperous management of money is scientific and formulaic, just like the rising and setting of the sun.

I believe the reason I passed the exam is the same reason you will not only get out of debt, but stay out of debt, make more money, and why you will not only save money, but learn how to enjoy saving it with minimum stress and distress. A new financial life and escape from emotional overspending first requires several shifts in your thinking. Let me show you how passing **"tests"** connected to real life money matters for me. We have all been tested by life's exams, hurdles, obstacles or problems, and such blocks seem to seriously diminish our ability to make and create the life we want. Passing this exam led me to the beginning of a reliable and adequate income, my financial tool, a blueprint, or building block for my future. This modest but steady income has been the foundation upon which I built my other activities as a real estate investor, a world traveler, and a business owner. I share this testing ordeal in my life so you can see how one decision, one position, or one experience can have a tremendous impact, either negative or positive, on your life. I went to an innovative training class; a class that caused a permanent <u>shift</u> in my way of thinking about and approaching "test taking." I have passed every test taken since the first time. Before the test preparation workshop, I operated out of the conventional wisdom that I would pass the test if I studied harder and longer.

I spent all this time "prepping" and studying, thinking that alone would get me the biggest reward—passing the test. You know the feeling. Am I alone? Raise your hand, if you are with me! We live in our emotions so much that we feel "spending" a lot of time on a task will lead to reward and positive results. If I spend a lot of time on the task, I will finally get it "right." I will deserve to pass! In a similar way you once believed that if you spent a lot of money on an object that it would offer you both better quality and more pleasure than something less expensive. Sad to say, no matter how many people in our society believe such obsolete paradigms, believing outdated paradigms does not make them true. That testing workshop helped me shift my feeling and thinking paradigms about the test and permanently freed me from an unfruitful way of looking at the experience.

This shift allowed me to move on in my life with high hopes, strategies for success applicable even when confronting life's crucial examination. Once our thinking shifts to an inward, heartfelt view of the new and true paradigm, your behavior will shift accordingly, usually permanently. You may be feeling that life is not fair; money is distributed way too unequally! You weren't born with that silver spoon in your mouth. You didn't have good training at home. Because I had the benefit of a clever and wise grandmother with good financial acumen, I have had fewer pains in my money life than some of my friends.

Not true, I've just had money pains of a different kind. I was in a co-dependent relationship where I gave away enough money to buy another house. You were better than I, in the sense that you benefited personally from your spending in that moment. Pain is common to us all. I am reminded of an analogy my friend Lisa used today to describe this journey we humans are taking together. We all leave from the same place at the same time, traveling in the same direction to the same or similar destination. When I get to the stop light, I get the red light and she does not. Why did I go on to catch all the red lights and he didn't get stopped by a single one? Why can two people have the same hometown, similar families, identical educations, and yet one looks like a great success in life and the other seems to flounder for years?

My colleague took the same test prep class, talked the entire time and still passed the exam on her first try. My test success took four separate attempts and a lot of anguish. We had the same degree, worked for the same company, did the same work, and yet had totally different experiences with the same test. Yet, at the end of the day we still wound up earning the same salary. Our financial achievements have been different as well, as she is struggling with fear of losing her home and I have not faced any financial challenges with property upkeep, even during the financial downturn. The paths we take may be quite different, but we can all end up with the kind of success we seek. Hey, you are saying, you failed that test! What makes you qualified to teach and write a book about money matters and money management for the sole purpose of helping working people who want more abundant lives? Well, my failures have taught me a great deal. For one thing, over several years I too have had to seriously question and rethink common societal assumptions. I took for granted my relationship to the money I earn each month and how I used or gave it. I am being transparent when I say that I have "shifted" my thinking into more conscious ways of looking at and handling money.

I have been blessed to have an uncanny gift to manage and grow money well and even with all my emotional giving, I have never suffered any real financial losses. My losses have been emotionally painful and often that is because I did not realize that I was being tested and failing yet again in area of "emotional peace." I have adopted, practiced, shared, and seen these five new "paradigms" work successfully in changing the way I and other people think about their relationship between money and happiness, emotional overspending and true giving. The result has been that I have been able to go on to use my money tools more effectively and to build what I believe is a life of wealth and well-being today. Admittedly, I struggled a lot emotionally, but I am convinced that I have learned the nature and emotional connection to the money test in life and how to pass it. I would venture to say the emotional factor is the most prominent reason we mismanage our money. And I can show you where to begin changing your own money feelings, thoughts and behaviors and how to go on building your own life of wealth and well-being, no matter where you find yourself at the moment. Just as there are formulas and strategies for passing exams, the same is true when it comes to personal finance, consumer spending and money management "tests".

There are cycles and forces at work that you may or may not be aware of that are impacting how you spend your money. In fact, I believe money is a tool and how we wield this tool impacts the quality of our lives. You've got to be aware in order to play the game differently and win the prize. Had I not changed my approach to taking tests, I do not believe I would have ever passed and my life would have taken a different turn. I am here to help you pass your "money test" by offering tips that have helped me, an ordinary and unlikely person, to achieve financial success and live a great life on a "small" salary. I believe these tips will help you achieve the financial success you seek. My modest accomplishments in educating myself financially and putting good strategies for success into place may inspire you to greater heights. No matter where you start or how fast you travel, the sky is the limit! As you have seen, thus far in our discussions we have focused on beliefs about money. I feel strongly that even one unquestioned, hand me down money belief can undermine all that you strive to do in your financial life. The five paradigm shifts we have reviewed here, when placed in your consciousness clearly and with conviction, will revolutionize your entire relationship to money. Let's look at them together here and pause to reflect on each one as well as the many resonances between them.

Paradigm Shift #1 introduces the fundamental revolution in your money thinking. Money is not emotional salve to heal your daily wounds or a brace to bolster your self- esteem. Money is your power tool. Train yourself how to use it well. I will share strategies I've used that may serve you well on your financial journey.

Paradigm Shift # 2 challenges you to consciously reject the common assumption that you do not now have enough. Really focusing on and accepting the belief that you are enough and that you are grateful for your current financial resources abundance can change your financial destiny totally, leading to increase in financial and emotional wealth.

Paradigm Shift # 3 starts with the widespread belief in our culture and others that money makes one happy. But the shift is a brilliant ray of light for your life. How much money you have and how happy you are in your life are not linked, once you reach a certain income. You can choose to have a wealth of happiness, no matter the amount of your paycheck.

Paradigm Shift # 4 suggests the surprising idea that **feeling** wealthy can be the starting place for **being** wealthy. The implications of this idea are enormous and shocking. If you feel like you do not have enough in your life, you will not have enough in your life, even if you had millions of dollars. If you operate your business from a belief that you do not have enough capital, you will not have enough capital. If you feel poor, you are very likely allowing your mind and behaviors to express themselves in poverty. Feeling and thinking you are rich will empower you to take actions to make yourself rich, rich in a way unique to you.

Paradigm Shift # 5 asks you to give up the conviction that repeating your hard work over and over yields success. Instead, explore the implications of the revolutionary idea that different action is required to achieve a different result. If all your hard work has resulted in financial distress, then more hard work is unlikely to remedy the situation.

Your new wealthier life may actually invite you to work less and enjoy more while you employ your money tool in new and more productive ways. Unlike conventional financial and consumer wisdom, I do not believe in, nor live a life of deprivation and severe sacrifices for myself, nor do I advocate it for others. I simply believe in taking a strategic approach to spending and managing money to ensure that I am getting the things I desire most, financially and personally. My finances are spent creating meaningful experiences that lead to a life well-lived, a life full of meaning and joyous stories I can pass on to my unborn children and their children to inspire and promote a sense of purpose. Essential questions for us all are: "Are we living and modeling a life of purpose? " "Is this the life of our dreams?" Sorry to say the answer for most of us is "No." I believe that we will answer these questions differently as we continue to read and learn.

REFLECTION: Which of these paradigm shifts resonated most and why? How can a shift serve you on your financial journey?

CHAPTER 4

THE EMOTIONAL PULL
ON YOUR MONEY

In the field of personal finance, money managers hardly ever focus on EMOTIONS, the powerful forces that drive so many of us to overspend, overconsume, and over-give. In addition, over-giving is hardly discussed in money management guides, yet it is a growing phenomenon, not only in the United States but around the world. It was the kind of overspending that I had to conquer. For me excessive giving was and still can be an emotionally charged stimulus, though impulse spending, impression spending or keeping up with the Joneses and comparison shopping are the frequently cited reasons for over-spending; often without a critical understanding of the deep emotions that underscore these behaviors, behaviors that keep many living in devastating debt. This understanding of emotional spending is absolutely necessary to making meaningful and maintaining lasting, effective financial paradigm shifts.

An example from my own life has shown me how real, how powerful, emotional factors like needing connection to others is and how it can lead some of us to "over-give." In fact, this longing to connect by way of my giving money led me down a painful path of disappointment and huge initial remorse. There were people in my life that I gave, gave, and gave money to in an effort to help, support, and bond. They were family members. They were good friends. They were loved ones. Sometimes I found myself paying their bills, making "loans", buying presents in an effort to win their love, loyalty, and support. Unbeknownst to me at the time, I desired to feel more wanted and accepted. After tumultuous and disappointing events and co-dependent work with Stephanie and others, I eventually came to see what was motivating me to use my income this way. It became clear to me I was trying to buy love and buying love did not work. It never works. However, giving money like this can leave us emotionally and/or financially broke.

Well-known financial gurus don't seem to talk very much about the role of emotions in our money difficulties. To me emotions are an important component of money matters and are at the core of how and why we practice certain destructive or self-sabotaging financial behaviors. I call the social phenomenon emotional overspending, and it is deeply embedded in the spending habits of our world-wide culture. I first discussed this on a larger scale in Dorothy "The Organizer" Breininger's book, Stuff Your Face or Face Your Stuff. There, I posed the question, "If the love of money is the root of all evil, then could emotional spending (overspending) be the root of all money woes?"[4] New research data shed light on this relatively new concept of emotional overspending. Data from the sciences are beginning to confirm my experience that our emotions act as partners in our spending practices or habits.

New research in the area of neurotransmitters examines how our brains work and how our hormones govern chemical functions in our bodies. According to this research, the brain's chemical functions are controlled by messengers called neurotransmitters. Exploiting the science of neurotransmitters, corporations and advertisers have come up with new methods of advertising and marketing called neuro-marketing. In an online news magazine, ISPO News, an article entitled "90 Percent of All Purchasing Decisions are Made Subconsciously" speaks to the challenges we are facing. The new science of marketing is used to encourage us to spend more, more, and more. This article tells us that this form of marketing science "studies consumers' sensorimotor, cognitive, and affective response to marketing stimuli with psychology."[5]

In other words, advertisers use these data to determine how we feel and think about the products they are selling and how to entice us to buy. On this topic of psychological manipulation, I recommend the works of Daniel Kahneman, a remarkable interdisciplinary scholar in both economics and psychology. In his Nobel Prize winning 2011 book, Thinking, Fast and Slow, Kahneman suggests that there are two powerful motivating factors or systems that influence purchasing decisions. One influence is lack of awareness or mindfulness during purchase. Lack of awareness results in "fast" decisions or what my Big Mama would call "eyes closed wide and in a hurry decisions." Without mindfulness during a purchase, one is most likely engaging in emotional overspending.

The second approach to buying is just the opposite. The second is "slow" thinking, which is associated with conscious deliberation and reasoning. A purchase based on a deliberate, "slow" approach to spending, usually involves a cooling off period between initial consideration of the purchase and the actual purchase, and requires the involvement of logic and reason. Impulse purchasing is based on emotion and mindful, planned purchasing is based on rational thinking and logic, even if the planned purchase is made for pure pleasure or diversion. This distinction between "fast" spending and "slow" spending is crucial to your progress in financial transformation.

Corporations around the world engage in deliberate attempts to influence our desires and extract as many hard-earned dollars from our wallet as possible, especially by inducing "fast" purchases. Millions of dollars are being spent to study you, to figure out how you think, what you like, and how to entice you to buy something whether you need it, use it, or want it. Millions are spent by these giant companies to make you a mindless, constantly craving, "fast" and obsessive consumer of goods and services. You have to train yourself to resist such manipulations and become a "slow" and strategic spender of your dollars.

The larger term used for this field is neuro-economics, an academic field in which expensive research is conducted and great intellectual effort is made to understand and determine what makes your brain tick—what makes you not only shop, but shop to excess. These scientists study us to determine just what we crave, how much, how often and when, even why. Then, what we crave is delivered at a price point which will fill the corporations' coffers. Neuro-economists look at deep motivations that cause us to engage in impulsive purchasing behaviors which lead to low rewards, few benefits, and huge debt. Even something as simple as the colors in a magazine ad can have a powerful impact on your purchasing decisions. Have you ever wondered why certain colors are used in department stores and others in grocery stores? The science of neuro-economics has taught corporations that deliberate and powerful color selection is central to their clever marketing campaigns.

Much marketing strategy is based on the idea that wired into the human psyche is emotional response to different wavelengths for color which stimulates actions like salivation in a movie theater lobby or sensual arousal in the lingerie store. Color selection in stores, hotels, entertainment venues, a neuro-marketing method, plus extreme repetition, as many as 5,000 ads per day, are just two of the manipulations which may be triggering your unplanned "fast" spending decisions, our so called retail therapy. Colors are carefully considered based on the actions the advertiser would like you to take or the feelings the merchant would like you to experience. Business Insider's Talia Wolf in an article entitled, "How Different Colors Are Convincing You to Buy Things" shares insight and the following chart on how the human brain is triggered by and wired to respond to color. Color selection is used to capture our attention and persuade us to not only take the action of buying something but also to do so in a particular way. Wolf suggests that marketers believe every color on the color wheel evokes a different mood or feeling. While color responses can be very subjective and vary from culture to culture, some colors appear to have a nearly universal meaning.

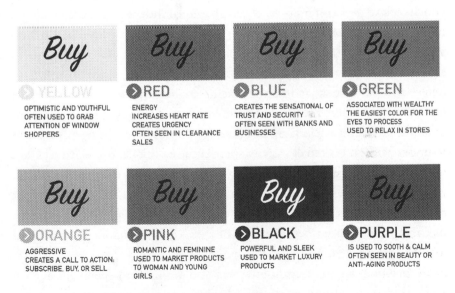

Color Chart is provided by Kissmetrics.

For example, psychological research studies have found that people exposed to the color red feel stimulated to react with greater speed. Just to illustrate how use of one basic color can have a powerful influence on you, look at the next store you are in or the next ad you see in a magazine.

Notice. Neuro-marketers have learned how to select a particular color to accomplish a specific goal when appealing to you. For example, you will very likely see red in the clearance section of most department stores. Studies reveal that red is experienced as a warm color all over the world. The color red is seen as an energy color that increases heart rate and creates a sense of urgency. You must buy this now! Red signs and red tags are everywhere in the clearance aisle. If advertisers want to appeal to our emotional need to feel wealthy, they use the color green. Green is easy for the eyes to process and relaxes us while we are shopping. Colors are used to manipulate us to spend impulsively and emotionally, rapidly satisfying our urge to comfort ourselves with a purchase.

Colors are used by outlet malls and fast food chains to separate us from our money. Orange is considered an aggressive color because it creates a call to action: subscribe; buy NOW. It seems to send us a friendly, welcoming, and upbeat message making us feel positive and encouraging us to take action immediately. Supersize that! Orange boldly tells us to buy it, right now! Brands which seek to project a friendly, cheerful, and confident personality may use orange in their corporate livery and on their websites. Outside of our awareness we are continually bombarded with color messages in fast food outlets, malls, signs for clearance sales, print ads, television commercials – and they call, loud and clear, for us to make an impulse purchase right then or at least next time we have the opportunity. I insert this information to show you how unconscious and how powerful a feeling or thought in response to something as simple as a single color can be. Small wonder we become emotional over-spenders. We are encouraged to get emotional and to overspend at every turn, in every store, in every restaurant, on every street corner and to do so quickly. Think about all the other tools in an advertiser's bag of tricks…. catchy jingles, sexy images, discount signs, mouthwatering images of food, celebrity endorsements, appeal to our desire and emotional need.

Obviously, we must go into stores and we have to spend money on food, clothes, gasoline, and many other things in order to live. When we do so strategically, rationally, with a "slow" purchase, we are likely to be managing our emotional selves and our financial lives successfully. But when we don't pay attention to these kinds of influences on our behaviors, our spending can lead to piles of things we do not need or use, eventually to the pain of **debt weight**. It is imperative to our own emotional and financial well-being that we become aware of and fully appreciate the power of neuro-marketing over our purchasing behaviors and begin to take more control of our thinking and movements when in commercial settings.

I ask you again, "If the love of money is the root of all evil, then could emotional spending/overspending be the root of all your financial woes?" This question feels a lot like asking "Which came first, the chicken or the egg?" Are we spending money on things that make us feel good or do we feel good just because we spend money? In other words, is our spending about the stuff we purchase or is there something else going on in us? Emotional overspending is most visible in what we call retail therapy. Emotional overspending refers to the belief that we can somehow spend our way to feeling good or we feel good when we spend. Chicken or egg? Buying something seems like an easy, convenient and even harmless way of soothing feelings of anger, guilt, depression, sadness, low self-esteem, fear, doubt, insecurity, anxiety. Spending seems to make us feel happy, alive, connected, and seems to make us forget about our problems. In short, buying can affect one in much the same way addictive drugs or alcohol can affect one. Buying stuff can get us "high." At least for a short period of time.

Advertisers try to convince us that a product or service is the answer to all our problems, our "fix." They hope to convince us that their product or service can bring us joy, confidence, status, and desirability among colleagues, friends, and potential mates. Shopping and spending may seem like a kind of therapy since it helps you take your mind off your problems or uncomfortable feelings for a moment; but it is a therapy that morphs into a mere temporary escape with sometimes financially disastrous consequences. Often, after the shopping spree ends, our uncomfortable or painful feelings soon return. Perhaps we end up feeling even worse because we start to feel guilty, out of control, and full of fear of the consequences of overspending.

But the next day, next week we go right back to the store, like the alcoholic who looks for more of his drink of choice. None of us enjoy the idea of being compared to an alcoholic, but the behavior of overspending is similar to addiction. Sometimes, the emotional over-spender is looking for a *fix* to fill some void in her psyche or ease some pain in his life, and as time passes, more clothes, more cars, and more stuff fail to satisfy the emotional need. In fact, more shopping results in less and less pleasure over time, but that doesn't mean that we stop seeking the spending "fix."

The desire to belong and feel important is another reason we engage in emotional overspending or retail therapy. Emotional overspending makes us feel popular, loved, and special within our community. There seems to be this growing belief that we are not enough or we don't measure up in and of ourselves, and somehow if we spend more, give more, then we will become more. If we drive the same car as our neighbor or a more expensive one, then somehow we have suddenly arrived. If I buy my friend this item or give this family member money to pay a bill, I will be accepted and liked. Yet we will always come up short and the huge corporations and their advertising agencies continue getting richer and richer. This vicious cycle works for them, but it does not work for us, the consumers. One of the richest men ever, Aristotle Onassis, said "Millions do not always add up to what a man needs out of life." The same holds true for us; more money and consuming more stuff do not satisfy the longing to be connected or fulfill any other emotional need for very long. I do not want to minimize the emotional need to connect and even help loved ones.

Research reveals over-giving is a growing phenomenon, problem around the world because of recent global financial challenges. Parents, in particular, offer more and more support to struggling offspring who find it hard to house and support themselves because of the difficult economy. Brothers and sisters rely more on successful siblings for financial help. Because I wasn't buying products, I thought this kind of spending was alright. But I learned from painful experience and Stephanie's wisdom that I wasn't investing in healthier relationships or helping anyone as I thought. Generosity and kindness when another is in crisis is fine.

However, you must make "slow" giving decisions by examining your own motives for and patterns of giving as I was led to do. Feeling good or connection (at some level) is what we all seek when spending and giving. And those huge corporations and their advertising agencies know how to make us think that a purchase will give us that good feeling we seek. Those 5,000 ads we are exposed to every day tell us shopping for various things is a diverting pastime. Malls are presented to us like huge amusement parks with all the trimmings; music, rides, movies, foods galore. People try on clothes and spend feverishly around us. Salespeople tell us how good we look in that wonderful cashmere coat. We may feel like a star for just that moment.

But, eventually, we are forced to face the budgetary consequences of retail therapy and emotional overspending. Your debt starts to increase and the bill collectors start calling. The shopping bills are due and so are bills for the essentials of food, utilities, and shelter. Emotional over-spenders often find they acquire luxuries and skimp on necessities. This kind of stress is bad enough if you are single and supporting only yourself. But what of the guilt and pain of the bills, the skimping, the deprivations when you have a mate or children relying on you for their well-being also? The real problem with overspending is excess, as the prefix "over" suggests. As with most "excess", pain and regret are the direct results. Here's the question we have to focus on. How do we break the cycle of excess and financial pain which arises from emotional overspending? How can we battle the pernicious influences of the neuro-marketers as we go through our days? Clearly, we can't escape the whirl of colors, ads, catchy jingles and celebrity sales pitches that surround us. How can anyone get out of this societal neuro-trap?

Obviously, some people in the world do manage their spending rationally, balance their budgets, and invest wisely for a life of security and happiness, so it must be humanly possible to protect yourself. The answer to protecting yourself from the pernicious influences of our present marketing demons can be found in neuro-plasticity. That is why implementing the five paradigm shifts we have identified is so crucial to creating new money behaviors in your life. Your brain is actually able to change, to make new connections which lead to new emotional links, to new thinking patterns and to new behaviors. Science suggests that you can strengthen your brain and thoughts like you would your physical body or muscles.

You can build up your mental financial muscles by learning new things, habitually practicing the new things, and rigorously embracing them. The goal here is to rewire or reprogram the brain for financial success by being mindful of your spending and the emotions which underlie your spending behaviors. Reshaping your brain can lead to valuing your passion and your life purpose more than you value the continual acquisition of things. In other words, your desire to fulfill your life's dominant passion can become more important than spur of the moment purchases and your short term goals. This possibility of purposeful change is really good news for every emotional over-spender, including those like me, who may be guilty of being the financial enabler for friends and family members. Change your emotions and thinking—change your life.

Now don't be afraid. You don't have to take a vow of poverty! I do, even, recommend you enjoy life while paying down debt and being a good money manager. It is possible to balance pleasure and financial savvy. In fact, it is also possible to find great pleasure in your life while limiting spending, or using "strategic spending" as I like to call it. Can you now sense emotional triggers that make you shop to excess? I didn't go wild buying brand names or high ticket items. But I did let my need to feel loved and connected take me down the garden path of giving too much to others. This is how emotional overspending manifested itself in my life and damaged my own personal well-being and financial peace for a long time and caused me a lot of disappointment and pain. Once we become mindful of our overspending triggers, we can take deliberate and concrete actions to avoid or change them; we take contrary action; i.e. do something different. You know how we go to a Farmer's market for fresh produce and fruit to maintain our physical health. Well, I would like this book to serve as a "financial farmacy" where you can find wholesome brain food and practical support for your financial health. What specific action do I recommend?

REFLECTION: Given the new research in neuro-marketing, how can knowing this help you spend differently? Think about certain feelings or thoughts that trigger you to spend emotionally or impulsively. List.

SOLUTIONS TO THE EMOTIONAL & PHYSICAL ACT OF OVERSPENDING

Admit that you are an emotional spender. The first step to solving any problem is to recognize and acknowledge you have a problem. Only then can you find a solution. Do not beat yourself up about spending because we are encouraged to do so by advertisers, sometimes family and friends, and a global consumer society. We have learned to soothe our feelings by acquiring things. We get caught in the trap of translating our feelings into consuming. Learn the lessons offered here, then forget about the past and move forward and enjoy the new relationship with money and wealth you're starting to build. Create and continue to practice these new habits. Repeat, repeat and add to the healthy new habits suggested in this resource. It only takes around 21 days to build new habits when focused.

Be mindful of and engaged in all financial activities, spending, banking, saving, investments, etc. Know what's happening with your money. Internally embrace conscious purchasing. Make each purchase a "slow" purchase. Obviously, in the face of a situation where you wish to purchase impulsively, slow down. Wait. Go home. Think. Examine your motives. Be strategic and calculating with money. Weigh the value of such a purchase. Only after such reflection, purchase or do not purchase. Write out a list of needs before going to any store. Limit yourself to those things on the list. If you realize you "need" something else, add it to the list for your next visit.

REFLECTION: Write 1 solution you can implement today, tomorrow, next week…

Go to website, NewFitWorldTV.com for blog, videos, and more on managing emotional overspending.

CHAPTER 5

MONEY THROUGH THE AGES

"The greatest discovery of my generation is that a human being can alter his life by altering his attitudes." William James

I am not a financial spiritualist who wants to overwhelm you with talk about the emotional psyche. However, there must be a shift in one's feelings about money which in turn will lead to changes in your thinking and eventually lead to changes in your behaviors as they relate to money, lifestyle, and the things you hold dear. A paradigm, as we have discussed, refers to a belief system, value, or thought pattern that may not actually be true; in fact, a paradigm may not even be conscious. Yet a paradigm is a mental construct which shapes our behaviors and can have a huge impact on how we live life and can even determine the very quality of our lives. How we feel and think determine what we do while we are growing wealth and what we will do when we actually get it. These same belief systems and patterns can send us into a downward spiral or keep us in the status quo, stagnant, where we are not growing in abundance but remain in an ongoing state of lack or living without the basic comforts, much less the abundance we deeply desire.

So when research tells us that 96% of our behavior and 90% of our spending is controlled by the subconscious mind, it is prudent to ponder, study, understand, and shift our financial state of mind in certain areas. For our purposes the <u>mind consists of our feelings, thoughts and actions</u> and a shift here can be quite powerful and over time increase our financial resources and abundance in every aspect of life. It may sound to you like I am saying we can think and grow rich. Well, yes, in many ways I agree with Napoleon Hill's "Laws of Success" and Rhonda Byrne's "Secret." However, in order to grow rich I believe we must consciously <u>align our feelings, thoughts and actions</u> to yield abundance in our lives.

The concept of paradigm shifts is the foundation of such an endeavor. The five paradigm shifts about money that I have invited you to move into are the beginning of your own transformation into a new state of mind about your relationship to your money. And that new state of mind is necessary to build the behaviors that lead to the abundant and happy life each of us seeks.

Paradigm shifts are not new; in fact many of them have taken place on a large scale and have had great impact on how we view the world and govern ourselves even today. If you take a look at the world we live in today—you immediately realize it is quite different from the world hundreds of years ago. The beliefs we hold about science, money matters and more, have evolved as well. Take a look at how our thoughts have shifted from old to new paradigms in the planetary or scientific realms. Moving from the belief that the earth is flat to the belief that the earth is round represented a huge paradigm shift at a certain point in time, though it is widely accepted and unquestioned today.

There was also a time when the prevailing thought was that flying machines were a preposterous notion; human beings will never take flight. Today, airplanes and helicopters are common modes of transportation. Spaceship vacations may be next! Scientific studies and technological innovations have led to huge shifts we now take for granted and behave accordingly every day. Just as our thoughts about scientific matters have shifted, it seems clear to me that our individual and collective ways of interacting with money have also changed over the years. To illustrate some financial truths, let us just take a moment to reflect on what I consider three very distinct periods in our global financial history. These periods represent certain beliefs and core paradigms that once served as the dominant way of thinking and to varying degrees, perhaps still shape our thinking and practices today with regard to money and wealth.

The three distinct periods or societies that shape our monetary beliefs and our financial practices most clearly are the following: The Agrarian Age, The Industrial Age, and The Information Age. The movement from one period to the next – from an agrarian society to an industrial society to today's information or technological society - brought enormous changes in the thinking and behaviors demanded of people in every culture of the world. Moving through such huge changes speaks to human beings' uncanny ability to adapt and adjust to their environment. In an agrarian society, most people lived on farms where sustenance came from the land. Working the land to earn your keep was standard and since profits from a farm tended to be scarce, bartering to some degree served as a form of currency. In the industrial world, we shifted from living off the land to living in big cities to working in factories, and manufacturing jobs became the new normal. The dynamics of big business and labor unions were born and led to huge struggles and achievement of better work hours, cleaner conditions, higher wages, health care, and retirement pensions, many of the compensations of being employed by a company that we still enjoy today, for the most part. The Middle Class was born. People often worked on one job for the long haul---25 or 30 years---and retired with benefits.

Today, we live in a world where technology is more prevalent than ever and where computers and the information they bring into our homes and workplace have become essential to our existence. Computer network specialists, web developers, programmers, coders, logicians, and those ubiquitous telemarketers are the jobs of today that did not exist in The Industrial Age. In today's Information Age, we rely heavily on "machines," especially computers, and tools like the internet, Facebook, and social media for our work, financial, and social lives. In some ways our culture appears to be shifting back to working at home again via computers and this Information Age.

Census.gov says "Working at home is on the rise, thanks to advances in communication and information technologies. Regular work-at-home among the non-self-employed population has grown by 103% since 2005. Employees, (3.7 million, 2.8% of the workforce) now work from home at least half the time."[6] In some industries, computers have completely replaced human labor. Work is scarce and job competition fierce, and you are no longer expected to stay on one job for 30 years. I had a conversation with a young millennial who is not even half my age, and it was shocking to hear her say that after only two years on the job her boss said he was surprised that she had been in that position for so long a time because that's uncommon in her industry and position. He wanted to know what her next career move might be.

Let's take a look at this economic transformation and its new thoughts and patterns from the perspective of money management. Each of these huge changes in social and economic organization of our world could logically be expected to be accompanied by equally huge shifts in the way we see our work lives and our incomes and our wealth building efforts. But often people stay "stuck" in old feelings and belief paradigms without realizing that such views no longer fit the world around them. They need what I call a "new fit." For example, on the farm, hard physical work might indeed be key to one's financial success, but in the technological age hard work, certainly long hours and manual labor, may no longer be the main key to one's success. Ask Mark Zuckerberg or Bill Gates how much of their success depended on manual labor. We will examine keys to success in a later chapter when we look at our gifts and talents as ways to increase wealth. I argue that our "mother's wit" regarding our personal and consumer finances has changed as well. My mother didn't have to deal with constant offers of credit cards in the mail or offers on college campus, for example, like so many of us are bombarded today. We must have strategies in place to overcome spend, spend insinuations and obstacles.

Yet, there are elements from each period that can be quite valuable to us as well today, if we are aware and choose to implement them appropriately. While I am a back to basics kind of girl in some ways, I think we can take the best from each period and use what suits and better yet, grows us in today's financial world. For example, the Agrarian Age represents a time when we were a less credit dependent society where sharing resources and bartering were prevalent. If a poor farmer needed a bushel of corn or a barrel of flour, he could borrow it directly from a more prosperous neighbor or perhaps barter his extra peas for corn. With industrialization came more need for government currency, banks, doctors, lawyers, factories and factory workers. But some people were still stashing their money under the mattress or in a tin can buried in the barn, wary of banks! For many no paradigm shift about handling their money accompanied the huge shift in the organization of the world around them.

Agrarian Age 1700s	• Bartering & Exchange • Farming Society • Sowing and Reaping
Industrial Age 1820s	• Pay before you play • Delayed Gratification • Strategic Spending • Beginning of City life • Gainful Employment • Saving/Saving Clubs
Information Age Late 1900s to present	• Consumers' Mentality • Buy Now, Figure it Out Later! • Credit Card Debt

For my grandparents in the early 1900s, various savings assistance programs were in their infancy. Fast forward to the 1970s and early 1980s, some banks still offered special Vacation and Saving Clubs. I remember my grandparents putting money in an account weekly to ensure we had a great Christmas and summer vacation. Big Mama always had what I call a "Fund Your Desire Account" which she maintained separately from her conventional savings account. I remember a time when Big Mama and even I knew the bankers by name, and they would personally offer us financial services that would make us more financially literate and sound. How about lay-away plans, virtually unheard of today? It is a method of purchase where the merchant puts a product on hold while buyers make payments. When item is paid in full, the buyer takes the product home. Like my grandmother, I have an account which I think of as my "Save for My Desire Fund."

I recommend you have one as well. Use this fund or account to purchase those big ticket items like concert tickets, summer vacations, designer gown, motorcycle, or any heartfelt desire. Once banks actually helped us think ahead and save for these experiences and a host of other things. It seems to me that just a few decades ago there was an atmosphere in which banks and stores actually supported a consumer's desire to save over time and purchase what she desired slowly, with care and deliberation. It was common for consumers to actually appreciate delayed gratification in action. I think we consumers fared better financially as well. While people may have had credit cards, there wasn't today's overwhelming reliance on a dozen lines of credit to keep one's life afloat.

The Industrial Revolution also represents a shift from hand production to mass production by manufacturing and machines. This shift led to new inventions and a move to big cities where incomes and the standard of living increased to varying degrees, eventually leading to the rise of the middle and upper classes in large numbers. Concepts of delayed gratification and pull yourself up by your own bootstraps were introduced, and Horatio Alger stories and rags to riches tales became popular sources of inspiration. Banks and Financial institutions continued to grow and grow in size and influence, leading to the formation of the New York Stock Exchange, international megabanks, and the FDIC guaranteeing the risk to our money with subsidized insurance up to a specific dollar amount.

I would suggest that the bank with which you are familiar today is quite a different bank than your mother's bank. Imagine a bank like those of old which actually attempted to help you save for your desires and actively encouraged you to manage your money, spending more strategically and carefully. Today your bank is more likely to offer you another new credit card, a debit card, an ATM card and a high interest car loan, if your credit rating is high enough! I think it is safe to say that today your banker is not your best friend, but she doesn't have to be your enemy. While he is certainly not as kind as he has been in recent times, it is a very good idea to be on friendly terms with your neighborhood banker.

Because of our computerized culture in the twenty first century, we may not even see our money anymore, much less need to hide it in the mattress. We may not even visit our banks, which makes it hard to form relationships with our bankers. Our direct deposits and automatic payments are making our checkbooks obsolete in the same way our phone landlines are becoming redundant. We need to shift to new views of our relationship to money which are in accord with the high speed computer age we live in. Our five paradigm shifts reflect some of these social and financial changes in the last few centuries. Let's think about the five new views of the world and money that I emphasize in this book as the basis of your movement toward financial transformation. First, the new paradigm that money is just a tool. Second, you have enough. Third, more money does not equal more happiness. Fourth, feeling wealthy is key to growing wealthy. And fifth, new action is required to achieve new results.

Reflecting on my childhood, I am stunned by how profoundly different our money lives are today. I cannot recall a time in my youth when my parents or people in general paid for a cup of coffee with a cell phone app, bought groceries with a credit card or shopped online for school clothes. Today, these things are the new normal! I remember going to major department stores where my mother could get a "lay away" plan with which she could make small weekly payments on a purchase until it was paid in full and then she could take it home. The Industrial Age represented a time where some people would save and save until they could pay cash for their cars and homes, a great example of using money as a tool and incorporating the other shifts as well.

In this Information Age my peers and I are more likely to bank online, review our statements, balance our accounts and pay our bills with our computers. We shop online where it is especially easy to shop mindlessly and increase debt and distress, without even the effort required of actual walking into the store. **Convenience can be costly!** We can have our payroll checks deposited into our account invisibly and have certain bills automatically deducted from it as well. Computers and cell phones make these tasks easy and save us a great deal of time. In truth, it is possible to live your life seldom actually seeing or touching a dollar bill.

Though we can bank online and connect with millions around the word, there are still some ways in which the computerized world makes life more difficult for us. For example, there is less connection to and communication with human beings or our own money. Life online can make it more difficult to build relationships with people who can give you specific guidance and immediate help in a financial crises. I build my financial relationships by actually going to the branch and regularly greeting my bank manager in a friendly way. Oftentimes, with just a simple hello and small talk. As a result, I have had bankers offer me exceptions to their rules, extend me credit without a credit check, and cash checks without my ID and money actual being in the account yet so that I could close escrow on a property in a timely manner. Beware of the potential isolating power of online banking, purchasing and paying. Though websites like mine and others can unite and empower us with fun money stuff, financial dialogue and knowledge, reliance on systems like this alone can disconnect you from people who may help fund your financial goals. The internet can sometimes be an illusion, can sometimes be an asset. It depends on how you pour the water.

Make every effort to communicate face-to-face and actual talk on the telephone. Though, we can connect with anyone anywhere in a matter of seconds which is also pretty remarkable by way of the worldwide web. Balance is key. I hope to impress upon you that managing and consciously connecting with your money should become just as routine as brushing your teeth and self-initiative is the vehicle to do so. Bankers used to help us be better managers by educating us and encouraging us to save. Today we have to be proactive in building relationship, acquiring money knowledge and money wisdom for ourselves in books, TV shows and websites, like New Fit World TV in order to be financially literate and live the abundant lifestyle we all desire.

The ball is definitely in our own hands, let me be clear. Merchants and bankers do not encourage us to be good money managers, and I am not sure what role, if any merchants should play in financial education. However, I believe bankers should offer us some educational opportunities where we learn to manage our money wisely and simple customer service to address an error or a problem, even though the financial banking paradigm has shifted to "You are on your own." Instead, the credit card system encourages us to "Buy now and figure out how to pay later." Today, many of us seem to engage in little planning, little saving, and little thought about the consequences of our spending habits. We are simply not taught their importance. Ouch! This practice enables banks and others to profit from the very financial mindlessness they encourage at every turn.

These institutions have found enormous wealth by charging us substantial fees just to get a credit card and renew it yearly. They charge us huge interest rates when we defer payments on our card payments and they charge us fees for taking our own funds from the ATM machine. I speak at length in my workshops about how to pivot and shift behavior to get the banks to be friendlier so you get what you want from them. Though "banking practices" sometimes contribute to our financial difficulties, technology also makes them convenient. In these busy times, conducting business online is a huge asset. We can perform a variety of banking activities anywhere and anytime. Of course, we must practice financial safety, protect our passwords and make them difficult to figure out. This technological age also offers vast stores of information, including good money management data that, are readily available and easily accessible to us. We can purchase any item we want from the comforts of our own home, huge assets to us busy money managers.

Yet, statistics reveal financial insecurity is growing globally and hope for abundance is diminishing among more and more peoples of the world. To me financial gain or loss is largely experienced first as an emotional matter, a result of fear and insecurity, lack of heuristic knowledge and a strategic plan. Steve Jobs was clear that the difference between people who prosper and people who don't is not intellect. This is why I stress strategic awareness of emotional factors, financial purpose, and savvy spending. Money should lead to financial security where you can be at ease knowing that your resources will last you at least one lifetime. You don't hear about this often, but for a short period after the recent economic meltdown spurred by the massive housing crisis, we Americans actually, though briefly, reverted to good money management techniques.

Then we went back to our old habits of mindless spending. John Kiernan cites the following statistics in his blog, "Ask the Experts: How Can We Improve Financial Literacy in the United States?"(May 27, 2014):

- Fresh off one of the worst recessions in history, U.S. consumers have racked up roughly $82 billion in credit card debt over the past 2 years and are on pace to bring amounts owed well beyond the $120 billion by the end of 2018.
- There is currently over one trillion dollars in outstanding student loan debt – far more than we owe either credit card companies or auto lenders. The average household balance as of 2010 (when the most recent figures were released) was $26, 682 and roughly 40% of households headed by someone aged 35 or younger owe money on student loans.
- More than a quarter of U.S. adults say they do not pay all of their bills on time, according to the National Foundation for Credit Card Counseling 2013 financial literacy survey. What's more, 60% of people do not have a budget and 40% give their knowledge of personal finance a grade "C" or worse.[7]

Yes, Kiernan's statistics show us the need for a paradigm shift in our society as a whole, a shift in the way we think, feel, and wield our money as similar problems exist around the world. These statistics also provide insight in what to do or "not to do" from era to era, or period to period so we don't find ourselves back in these individual and collective **"debt weight"** predicaments. So what can we learn from a study of these three historical periods? How will this information help us with financial success today? Change for the better starts with emotional and mental shifts. Actions follow. Shifts can begin with us taking time-proven success lessons, methods, or "best practices," as we say in education, from each period and using them to help us on the road to build sustaining and lasting wealth today.

We can begin this journey now regardless of our individual starting point. For example, The Agrarian Age represents a time when people worked collectively to achieve their financial goals, even if for the majority that meant simply keeping food on the table. I wouldn't be surprised to discover that the concept of potluck came from this era. I would also venture to say nowhere in history is the concept of sowing and reaping more evident than in The Agrarian Age. But of course nature and planting and harvesting and reliance on food for human life are timeless universals. We still rely on agrarians for our food today. The Agrarian Age, however, conjures a graphic when we can visualize and literally see people planting and growing their own food and we see an actual image of how growing our own food resembles growing our own money. Galatians 6:7b in the King James Bible states "...For whatsoever a man soweth that shall he also reap." In other words, the financial seed (good or bad) we plant is the specific seed that will grow. It is an agrarian truth that will last throughout the ages.

However, wholesome and nourishing crops do not grow overnight. Growth and abundant harvest take time! The second agrarian truth is that we always reap in kind. Sow the seed you want. Sometimes we forget that and sow seeds that give an undesired result. For example, if we plant apple seeds, we will reap apple trees. When it comes to our finances today, many of us think we are planting apple seeds while we dig a hole and throw in lemon seeds. Sometimes, that may not be a bad thing if we want to settle for just any fruit. But for those of us who want a specific fruit, a fruit we were born to plant and eat, and who desire the specific harvest we envision, then we have to invest the time to select our seed carefully and pay specific attention to the soil itself. We have to make sure the soil is fertile and remember to plant the proper seed. I repeat, "If you want an apple tree, make sure you are planting apple seeds."

Wanting apples and later discovering you've got oranges can be disturbing. I frankly do not want to settle anymore for just any fruit. But moving beyond that, statistics suggest we are killing our financial crops with overspending, scattering our seed on dead soil with absolutely nothing but massive **"debt weight"** as the result for our spending habits. Let me tell you a story that illustrates how this seed planting metaphor for our money applies in our lives today. A friend tells the story of a loving mother who would make cookies, cakes, and other baked goods to console friends and families suffering the loss of a loved one. She did it so often that she became famous for it in her community. One day this same mother died, and her community showed love by taking baked goods to her children.

The daughter complained the community did not support her mother. She was disappointed with the cakes and cookies. She wanted a financial gift, a seed her mother had not planted. She expected and preferred gifts of money! But her mother sowed the seed of baked goods and the warmth and comfort they bring. When this same mother returned to dust, her community gave in kind. So what's wrong with this picture? Nothing, if baked goods are all you want. However, her daughter wanted some other fruit to honor her mother. Moral of the story. **If you want financial success, you have to sow seeds that are consistent with producing financial wealth**. After you have acquired the seed, you must consistently do what it takes to prepare the soil, plant, care for, and harvest the corresponding return.

Just after my divorce, I had fallen on challenging emotional times, bought a house, and decided I wanted to nurture green grass instead of the brown turf that had overtaken my yard. Resurrecting my sad lawn was not easy to do, but I felt my efforts were therapeutic as I watered my grass daily. I thought I needed special equipment, but my mother (the smartest person I know) told me all I needed to do was water my lawn and it would turn green. That's all I did, to my neighbors' bewilderment. Apparently, I had become the talk of the block; see the crazy lady using an old fashioned water hose to water her lawn. She bends down, focuses on the dark spots then tends to the green areas to keep them green, and while meticulously focusing on turning the remaining stubborn brown patches green. My dedication became so apparent that it attracted attention. My neighbors wanted to help by lending me more modern equipment. They offered gardening advice, lawn care technique, and laughing support like "Hey, you missed a spot!" Pretty soon nearby sports fans were walking by and telling me that they could play football in my yard because I had the best grass on the block. I do not know much about football, but I took it to mean my grass was indeed great looking. It brought me a sense of pride and beautified my neighborhood as well as my house. The caveat here is that when I first asked my new neighbor for help with a big yard job, he declined support. However, when I demonstrated my desire and willingness to work independently, strive for success, this same neighbor and others volunteered support and their expensive yard tools. (I have learned it's best to stick to tools that are yielding the result you want.) They even watered the grass a few times in my absence.

Watering the grass seems like a small, little task, but to my surprise it had a big impact on my emotional peace and led to a great sense of community amongst my neighbors. The greatest lesson of my life is this and I believe it is universal and therefore will work for you. **Working towards your vision and purpose will attract people and resources, and financial prosperity follows, no matter how small the first step**. Attraction is a law and is no respecter of persons. My dedication inspired others to take better care of their lawns as now they too are watering their grass with a simple water hose. **Know thy money tools.** Like the simple water hose, small money tools and daily little steps can be very effective and take you farther than you could have ever imagined. Paying my bill on time each and every month for 6 years inspired a Banker to call a company on my behalf. To my surprise, the merchant told me I could have what I want at the price I want, per the Banker's request and support of me. I was floored and had no idea I could even ask for such a thing! I am so passionate about you finding the financial success you seek and I am writing this book to help you get it! I also give back to causes I strongly believe in and in doing so, I have found favor with another who is showing strong support for a special project in the works. Hang in there!

The support of others, bankers, neighbors, friends, family, will come when they see you working with care and commitment to achieve your goals.

People may not offer financial help per se, but it is very likely that they will support your vision and cheer your efforts to bring your vision into fruition when they see your dedication. Be encouraged, think about the financial seeds you've been planting and how you've been taking care of them. Have you been sowing into good ground? I am no farmer, but I have learned that good soil is as important as good seed. Do we need to pray for more rain or shall we start again in new soil to build your new financial life? Either is fine, but we just have to be up for and aware of the unique challenges each stage brings. The act of watering grass is relatively simple, but doing it daily and with precision requires concentrated effort and laser like focus. Sometimes, such caretaking feels like a lot of work and in the beginning it is, but once the system is in place, the activity takes less time and becomes less challenging. The hardest part is getting started. The mere fact that you are reading this book tells me you are looking for new soil in which to plant your financial seed and you hope for a great harvest season. In the words of Bishop T.D. Jakes, "Get ready, get ready, get ready!"

The Industrial Age was a major time of growth and innovation for the planet as well as for America. More people entered the work force as employees during this time than ever in our human history. The Industrial Revolution led to the rise of global cities, widespread employment in manufacturing of all sorts, and the growth of the middle class. As a history major in college, I learned that the Industrial Age led to what is called tertiary or sophisticated laborers in the work force as well as managers with higher education. The advent of new inventions like steam power, the cotton gin, electricity and the telephone and more shows the depths of creativity and "wit" that led to a new way of life where people moved to cities and then to the suburbs, and began totally new ways of living, new ways of being fruitful. I call it the era of "wit" and creativity; a time of invention. What "wit" and creativity has been stirring in you? The Industrial Revolution was a time where material riches and work productivity increased enormously for huge numbers of people, and the world prospered with a rapid rise in middle class wealth. Your grandparents, parents, and working people everywhere are likely the beneficiaries of the rapid expansion of wealth in our society-- able to own homes, cars, televisions, luxuries like refrigerators and washing machines unknown to those in The Agrarian Age. What inventions will you provide in this Information Age for the world to use and enjoy?

The Information Age created by the invention of computers and all the related technology has been an even more amazing transformation of the world. To me the best thing about technology is that we can communicate in new ways with people all over the world in a matter of seconds. I love and encourage use of all this technology because it's a way for us to connect and to support one another on our life journeys and do all kinds of great things together. Access to one another and a wealth of information is at our fingertips, just a click away. Even though our computer technology can distance us from our money in some ways and isolate us from others at times, it is still a huge asset to someone when used strategically to seek greater wealth in this life. I am not a technological person, but they tell me apps and creating new games can be lucrative. Do you have this kind of skill or know someone? Are you well-organized? Do you have a friend who is a gifted "procrasteneur" (procrastinator/entrepreneur with great ideas)? Think of how you can perform win-win partnerships. I encourage you to visit the website newfitworldtv.com and share your vision and perhaps find a muse, partner, and/or support group. Let's build and grow a fun financial community! The worldwide web is absolutely amazing in its ability to connect and provide access to people, resources, and information in mere seconds.

With the internet connection we can plan ahead for the next holiday season, set up a NO SPEND day, participate in saving challenges and organize and act as a financial/life community. Wouldn't it be fun to increase your financial well-being and success with a group of like-minded friends and fans? I encourage you to visit the website and get plugged in. We have instant connection to the ingenuity of others all over the world who post life building information for free. We have model instruments of growth and abundance, power tools for managing our wealth. We are still bouncing back from the sudden collapse of the American real estate bubble, and there couldn't be a better time than now to plant for a great new harvest. **Nothing spurs growth and creativity better than economic recession and pain!** Let's make some strategic shifts to join our minds, and catch up with the new powers available to us all and the powers that have been in us all. Let's also begin to see our finances as an integral part of our life. Let's move away from the tendency to separate our financial well-being from other aspects of life. In my blog, I wrote about how the body operates and functions as one, though there are numerous parts: arms, legs, feet, etc. When we shower, we don't think of washing an individual body part like the arm, but instead we take a holistic approach and wash our entire body without much thought in order to remain clean and healthy. Our financial life should be seen in this same vein. We need money! Money is a necessity. Adopting feelings and thoughts like these is as important as proper budgeting and other money management tools.

New York Times best-selling author of The Automatic Millionaire, David Bach, tells us that one of the most important things we can do to improve our financial lives today is to automate our relationship to money with conveniences like direct deposit of our paychecks and systematic payment of our regular bills. Like me, he believes that everyone in America (everywhere) needs to be offered better training before they become wage earners: "Financial education needs to be part of our national curriculum and scoring system."[8] While there has been some insertion of financial topics into school textbooks, we still have a long way to go, particularly in making topics personal, significant, and relevant to students' everyday lives. We often think about 3Rs when it comes to learning, but I submit there is a fourth "R:" in addition to reading, wrRiting, aRithemetic, and we've referred to it multiple times –Relationship.

Today we need a lot less math to steer our financial lives and a lot more Relationship. What do I mean by adding "Relationship" to our financial education? I mean that in western culture, there is still this concept of rugged individualism or the belief that we are lone rangers and we have to create our good life on our own—pull yourself up by your own bootstraps, a not so positive legacy of the Industrial period. The truth of the matter is that in today's Information Age and previous ages, nothing great and life changing happens by going it alone. I agree with the sentiments of the great Helen Keller, "Alone we can do so little, together we can do so much." The computer empowers us to connect with any resource or virtually any person on the planet in order to further our own knowledge and skill sets. New Fit wants to establish and maintain these kinds of relationships to help build a global life/financial community (family) as we transform ourselves to increase financial wealth and live the life of our dreams. Our schools should go beyond teaching us the mechanics of how to use the technology. More importantly, they could teach us more conscious use of our cyber power tools in managing our money lives and they should teach us to foster opportunities for global relationship building. Staying consciously "connected" is central to our own success, especially financially. The "Global Village" is here to stay. What happens here in the United States affects what happens in countries around the world and echoes to every corner of the world in seconds. The reverse is true as well. What happens in other countries affects us in the United States. We can affect one another by sharing our stories, our great finds or bargains, our witty money tips, and more.

A look at the achievements of the greatest men and women throughout history reveal they had help; they forged relationships and worked together to create new views of the world and new patterns of success. Jesus Christ Himself called twelve disciples, and each had a specific mission while together they transformed the world profoundly. Elizabeth Cady Stanton and Susan B. Anthony had the backing of hundreds of thousands of women, and wide support was critical to the transformations created by Martin Luther King, Jr. and the Civil Rights movement. Strong sustained relationships between committed men and women are key to creating the energy that transforms in profound and lasting ways. The same principles of helping, team work, and forging relationships can be applied to wealth building. **You don't have to go it alone**. We can form relationships to help and support one another's personal development and financial growth. Technology makes it possible for those of us still operating as emotional money managers to build community, share financial information which may make us better stewards of our resources. Building friendships in your community, your bank, stores, churches, schools while maintaining communication with people all over the world are excellent steps toward personal and financial success.

A paradigm shift may begin with one great mind like that of Copernicus, but ultimately to change the world the paradigm shift has to take place in you, me, and in our neighbors to change how we think, act, and achieve our goals. Sometimes, the shift starts with a huge scientific discovery or an amazing new invention, and sometimes the shift is more personal and powerful; a simple change in us, a simple change of heart and mind in the individual. Today, we look at the sun and school teaches us that it is our planet which is moving around it, not vice versa. Today, I feel like I am a farmer who is planting financial seeds and the ancient ages tell me if I water the seeds they will grow. But, I also have an entirely new kind of equipment to use and a new global community to support me in my financial farming that my grandparents could have never imagined.

Of course, this powerful system is a double edged sword. If I don't learn to use its new technology, I will be left behind in building my financial success. And worse yet, I must be mindful of the technological dangers of hackers and protect my password, financial/private information and guard where I go online. I must also be wary of how I can become so engaged with online life that I spend hours there browsing the internet, distracted and non-productive. Think of online shopping for example and how it can actually make emotional overspending even easier! Just one click of the mouse and I can spend a month's income.

Our five paradigm shifts to new ways of viewing money in our lives show us that money, like our computer technology, is just a tool to create the life we want. Our emotions and thoughts actually drive the way we employ our money tool. Money is not our ultimate goal in life. It is the byproduct of our pursuit of purpose. Our money is our means to our goal, and our goal is a life of true emotional and spiritual well-being enhanced by financial success and peace of mind. Let's take a closer look at this tool we call money and the vital role our thoughts play in its acquisition, management, and growth.

REFLECT: What lesson can you take from each age to help you on your financial journey?

CHAPTER 6

TWELVE GATES INTO THE CITY OF PROSPERITY. HALLELU.

**"You must learn a new way to think before
you can master a new way to be."**

**Marianne Williamson, contemporary
American spiritual teacher**

Like Marianne Williamson and other "new thought" guides, I strongly believe how we feel and how we think are the roots of our current financial standing, good or "not so good." Our money behaviors cannot help but follow our feelings and our thinking patterns. A discussion of popular money beliefs must be put in perspective if we are going to have good financial success. Some of these beliefs commonly held in our culture, some probably held by you, can severely hinder you on your path to financial well-being and need to be permanently discarded for real and lasting financial growth to occur. Our five "old paradigms" are such outdated financial beliefs. Discard them now. And move on. Move on to focus on the new ways of thinking as revealed from the "money eras" and that the paradigm shifts show you.

But where do you stand right now in terms of your financial thinking? We took a quick ten question quiz to identify connections between our emotions and our spending behaviors in the earlier Financial State of Mind quiz. Now I would like you to pause in our discussion and answer "yes" or "no" to each of the following ten questions regarding the actions you bring to money management.

State of Your Financial Thinking

1. Do you often feel desperate to get your next paycheck?
    Yes_____ No_____
2. Is your checking account occasionally so low that you resort to purchasing food with a credit card? Yes_____ No_____
3. Do you sometimes find you spent more than you earned in a pay period? Yes_____ No _____
4. Do you think of working overtime? Yes _____ No_____
5. Do you sometimes skip payments or juggle partial payments because you don't have enough to pay all your credit card balances? Yes_____ No_____
6. Do you often think you will never get "out of the hole"? Yes_____ No _____
7. Do you sometimes have to ask for a loan from a friend or family member to see you through to pay day? Yes_____ No_____
8. Has an unexpected expense like a car repair or medical emergency left you with no savings? Yes_____ No_____
9. Have you refused to answer the phone because of fear of collection agents or that a utility service may be cut off? Yes_____ No_____
10. Have you ever had a credit card cut up or refused when buying? Yes_____ No_____
11. Do you often assure yourself that financial distress will get better in time? Yes_____ No_____ TOTAL Yes_____ No_____

If you answer "yes" to four or more of these questions, it is very likely that your current state of financial status is in need of repair. This is a call to align your feelings with new patterns of not just thinking but practices that will be more consistent with attracting and maintaining abundance into your life. I am suggesting twelve new ways of being and doing with your money. These are changes that will allow you to begin to correct and stabilize your relationship to money and invite increase. In this chapter I identify and isolate twelve gates. Each is an entry into a viewpoint or practice which you might employ to better your financial status right now. I think the image of twelve gates into the city of abundance resonates deeply with those of us who seek a renewed way of living.

The number twelve plays a frequent role in the Bible and other facets of our daily lives that we sometimes take for granted. The symbolism of twelve is frequently used in association with a new beginning and new foundation and new structure. For example, stories of the twelve tribes of Israel and twelve apostles are well known starting points and principles of life. They serve as foundational "thought" and underpinnings of our world. In the Bible the tree of life bears twelve fruits. And our diurnal lives are patterned with images of twelve "new" intervals, a twelve month calendar and twelve hours on a clock. So let us look at each of the twelve "gates" through similar eyes. Each is a symbolic entrance into a new perspective or action, an opportunity to begin anew changing not just our thoughts and behaviors with money, but changing our very way of being in the world, including our "being" with money.

The twelve gates appear here in no specific order or hierarchy of importance. Like those twelve gates into the Holy City of Jerusalem, you may enter one and exit another at will, depending on individual need, interest, or growth level. They all provide access to the same wondrous city. In Biblical times, marketplaces were situated at gates, there buying and selling and other business transactions took place. Indirectly, gates may also be a place to hone one's gifts and let one's skill set shine in prosperous trade. May each gate into new thinking offer you entry into greater wealth.

In teaching circles we often craft individualized lesson plans to ensure students' academic success. Journals are kept to plan, record, and evaluate progress. As you explore these 12 gates, consider where you are and how you can modify your present thinking to get the most beneficial and immediate financial results for yourself. Create and write your own individualized pathways into your city of abundance. There is no one gate. There are lots of paths we can take to financial abundance, as it is defined differently for everyone, just as the dollar amount needed for each life varies. Implement whichever one appeals to you most or begin with whichever one seems to be most urgently needed. After reviewing all twelve here, just choose one or several and start on your way to a better financial state of mind and financial increase. Again, take immediate steps to work on the ones that are most necessary right now, and allow the others to be absorbed and implemented slowly. All the gates lead you into the same wondrous city, a place where you live like a millionaire.

To continue our metaphor of financial "sowing and reaping," we must remember that repeated actions become habit whether we intend them to or not. Whatever you sow, it does not take long for a fruitful seed or a pernicious weed to begin to root and fill the field before you. Remember research suggests it takes as little as 21 days of similar daily action to change, replace a habit or form a new one. Remember how powerful repetition used by those advertisers is! With repeated practice, in little over a year you would likely be considered an expert at anything you wish. This section will help you discard self-sabotaging practices or habits that keep you bound to a sense of lack. Reshape your thinking habits to prepare the fields of your life for the first seeds of long term wealth building or your increasingly wealthy life.

GATE ONE: Think "Time is Money."

Truth is, most of us do not devote much of our time to conscious caretaking of our financial lives. So, one of the first and most important behavior changes one can make to improve one's financial life is simply to **schedule more time to tend to it**. A garden which is seldom tended is likely to grow into a real mess and is likely to produce very little of value. The time you spend tending to your money is likely to pay off in producing more money. There are several important places to give your money life more time and special attention. Take the time to look at your paycheck slowly and carefully when you get it. Look at all the deductions. Look at your net take home pay. That net is all you actually have to work with and like "the little oil", it is enough. See if there may be ways you can increase your net. Are your tax deductions and medical provisions the appropriate amounts for your needs right now? Large federal and state tax deductions can be a kind of forced savings if you have difficulty putting money aside. On the other hand, with excess tax deductions you may be giving away cash that you have greater need for right now to help pay off credit card debt or pay for essentials. Speak to your tax advisor about the best approach for your personal needs right now.

Every month you also need to take the time to really see how much you have spent. Save your receipts every day; no matter how small. Put your receipts in one place, maybe a bowl on the kitchen counter, every evening for an entire month. Take an hour or two to sit down alone at the end of the month and go through all those receipts. List all your expenditures on a single sheet of paper, everything from rent and utilities to all food expenses, even those coffees in the gas station, and those one time purchases on your credit cards. How much did you spend this month? Compare what you spent to the net income you earned! Taking TIME to consciously identify what you earned and consciously total what you spent each month for the next three months is a good way to start seeing where your emotional overspending is occurring. Then take another hour to sit down and identify where you have an opportunity to exercise more awareness and start to tend to your weeds right away. Eliminate wasteful and unnecessary spending, and make it a lifestyle change or practice.

GATE TWO: Who says an Ant Can't… Move a Rubber Tree Plant?

The plan (thought) of the diligent leads only to abundance…. Proverbs 21:5

In grade school, story-telling time and in that classic old Frank Sinatra song, "High Hopes," the hard working ant is a model of an important kind of life wisdom. Sinatra tells us, "When your chin is on the ground, there's a lot to be learned, so look around!" Using our old paradigm, we tend to think the moral lesson is that the ant's hard work is what makes him an inspiration, but if you actually look at the stories and listen to the song, it is not at all the ant's hard work but his "HIGH HOPES," HIS ATTITUDE, which makes him a proper model for us! Remember our paradigm shift #4. In the twenty first century, hard work alone is not likely to make you rich.

Certainly, I would agree that there's a place for hard work in attaining financial success. Yet, I am also suggesting that hard work alone plays less of a role than we have traditionally been led to believe in the process of wealth creation. Your grandparents may have found it true that hard work was central to their fall crop on the farm. For your parents employed in an office or a factory, to some degree working hard from nine to five may have seemed to pay off with a mortgage on the house with the picket fence, two and one half children and a dog, and the car with 36 payments. But did all that hard work really offer your parents wealth?

Today, if you are still using the "hard work yields success" view of the world, you are even more likely than they were to end up finding "I did everything right, but I am still broke!" But why isn't hard work making you rich? Well, let's go back to the hard working ant. Ants are very peculiar insects. Have you paid attention to the pesky, yet determined and focused little creatures at the family picnic? They are very tiny shining examples of how to accomplish big goals. Like us, most ants live in huge colonies and their societies are characterized by division of labor, and teamwork----many members of the society working as one, with a high degree of focus and concentration----is central to the health of the hive.

The work done by one ant is just a tiny cog in the enormous social machine of collective survival. Some dig tunnels, some gather food, some remove waste, some are warriors; the queen just rules. Together their individual skills and work keep the society humming in good health and unity. True, an ant may not actually be able to move a rubber tree plant, but a worker ant can carry more than twenty times his own weight. Even then his hard work doesn't make him rich, but his every day focus, relationship/teamwork and absolute determination in his working does contribute to the harmony and survival of his entire ant world. An ant becomes a very successful contributor to his society.

If you look at any successful business person, you will see similar traits. People often talk about Steve Jobs' dogged determination to achieve. Could he have learned his intense focus from our pesky ant friends? Ants seem to have several other strengths that can also serve us well. It is not just hard work that makes their efforts so successful. Ants seem to work in harmony with the seasons. They store food for winter, i.e. they "save." They appear to have goals toward which their efforts are directed, and they appear to allow plenty of time to achieve those goals and they strive for their goals with seemingly endless patience. I ask you to find an "ant" or person, someone who shares a common vision and partner with one another or just help each other out. I have got a friend where we barter our time. For example, I help with her project for a couple hours and she helps me with mine for the same agreed upon hours. When you bring in just one additional partner your productivity doesn't just double but **quadruples**.

I believe for us the most inspirational part of an ant's behaviors is his discipline. He appears to go about his activities with utmost concentration.

Even more important than his hard work is the fact that the ant doesn't seem to get distracted and he isn't deterred by the occasional obstacle. Ants just figure out a way around an obstacle. Purpose driven, concentration, and persistence are three of the most important elements to employ consistently in your new financial behaviors. Let's learn from the ant and make each a habit.

GATE THREE: Make Yourself the Chief Executive Officer of Your Own Life

Ponder this gateway into a better financial life for a moment as it can alter the way you see yourself and your skill set for the better. Think about the work of the CEO of a successful national or international corporation. What does a CEO do? What makes him or her successful? A CEO has enormous responsibilities. He or she has to have lots of "wit" and heuristic knowledge, supporters, and resources to manage the overall operations of a large (once small) company. But keeping his head down and working from nine in the morning to five in the afternoon is not the key to his success. In fact, it is more likely that a CEO is on the job 24/7 in the early stages, as he or she wears many hats. The CEO of a business has to have, first and foremost, VISION. He has to see the whole financial picture and have a purpose in all his activities and a conscious goal toward which he moves. Generally, the CEO can express her purpose and goal clearly to herself and others and even better, she can oversee and motivate others to support her in achieving the mission.

A CEO constantly seeks wise counsel and diverse sources of input to ensure his own knowledge base. He constantly adjusts his decisions and behaviors in response to what he learns. A CEO also conscientiously monitors his own progress financially. He knows his inventory. She has certain benchmarks in place to monitor monthly, quarterly, or yearly progress and failure. A good CEO works out a five year plan, a ten year plan, and is always looking forward to sustaining his success for the long haul. If you are going to grow your financial life into long term wealth, you need to begin by appointing yourself Chief Executive Officer in charge of all your own money business.

This will be most effective and exemplified in your home life, where you manage the business of your household. You will find that your increased money management skills are transferable to your career and your investments. The CEO skills I have gained in managing my money life have helped me manage a successful real estate investment portfolio for almost 20 years. I have never taken a business class, though I study and read related materials for at least 30 to 60 minutes per day. However, I am sure such classes are of great value. What I have discovered through my own research is that many of our most successful business leaders were not necessarily A+ students and that a good many of them didn't graduate from college. They may not be any smarter than you or me. However, they may be more powerful planners and adept at implementing their goals. They may have extraordinary focus and determination. They take command of their own lives. Their success is intentional, not accidental. Starting now, we will do as our models of success have done. The buck will stop here, right on our own desk. Let us declare no more limits on our talent and potential. Let's take pride in where we are now and strive for even more where we are going.

Right now you may be not only the CEO but also the Chief Treasurer, Banker and Tax Accountant, Administrative Assistant, Social Media Rep. for your life, though you may soon find that reliable people with specialized expertise can be employed to help you with these areas as your wealth grows. For the moment, however, as you begin putting your new financial state of mind in motion, you will need to do most jobs yourself. You will need to manage your own employment duties well, you will need to manage care of your family and home, you will need to plan and execute a logical flow of money into and out of your life each month, and you will also need to anticipate dangers and reduce risks as you begin to grow financially. You may even think about starting your own company. Being the CEO of your own life doesn't require a business degree, but it does entail becoming a successful problem solver.

GATE FOUR: Buy Low: Live High!

People often think they need a lot of money to live a good life. I hope to prove to you that you can live a great life on your current salary, no matter the amount, when you strategically spend and consciously manage the dollars you have. In your new financial state of mind as CEO of your life business, you will no longer operate as an emotional over-spender, purchasing on impulse and ever-changing feelings without regard to long term consequences. Au contraire. Quite the contrary in fact. In your new financial life you are making the shift into new paradigms of conscious concern where long term value of and financial "return" on your purchase rule.

Obviously, I am offering you a bit of word play on the old stock market cliché of "Buy Low: Sell High." Read the Sports Page in your local newspaper, and you will find a talented young person who has just been offered tens of million dollars for five, six years of work. But note their millions often come with a few challenges and growing pains. What our newspapers don't usually report is that five years or so after retirement, the same person is declaring bankruptcy. Sports Illustrated did highlight this startling fact with an article in 2009 claiming that 78 percent of NFL players were bankrupt or facing serious financial distress within two years of ending their playing careers and 60 percent were totally broke within five years of retirement! Similar statistics are true for NBA basketball players and other professional athletes.

Young and lacking knowledge in money management, many sports and other entertainment celebrities with large disposable incomes overspend. They buy big houses, fancy cars and make unwise investments. **The payments outlast the income**. Working people like you and me hear such statistics and are perplexed. We think "That could never happen to me." Not so fast. It could. Take a look at the average lottery winner who suddenly comes into millions of dollars. The results are similar to the experiences of sports and entertainment personalities. According to Riches to Rags, in a 2010 study by researchers at Vanderbilt University, the University of Kentucky and the University of Pittsburgh, the more money you win in the lottery, the more likely you are to end up bankrupt. The old paradigms are at work here. If you are not a conscious and strategic money manager, the more you have; the more you spend.

But I am convinced that one old adage my mother used is still very true. She loved the wisdom coined by Benjamin Franklin. "A penny saved is a penny earned." A conversation I had with a family member comes to mind to bring it home. Before a recent Thanksgiving dinner we found it necessary to go to the grocery store at the last minute for seasoned salt. The choice in the store was between a brand name and the same generic product which cost one third less. My cousin's income is way less than mine, but she immediately reached for the most expensive seasoned salt instead of the generic brand I always use to make my world famous potato salad. Since I was paying, I insisted on buying the cheaper salt. Of course my seasoned salt came in a plain bottle, whereas the higher priced salt looked prettier in its fancy bottle. Would you rather pay less or pay prettier? Shifting paradigms. But I had to show her the label and convince her the ingredients were exactly the same in order to persuade her that I wouldn't be ruining our Thanksgiving side dish. She was, but I hope she is no longer, the victim of that old money paradigm, "If it costs more, it is better." I know this is simply not so. The value of a purchase is not equal to its price. For me value is determined by its utility and its quality and its contribution to my own personal satisfaction level in life, the gold standard.

But what of buying used or vintage things? I am a big fan of vintage shopping at thrift stores, garage sales, flea markets, farmers' markets and parking lot sales, and outdoor markets around the world. In these places you can buy the things you like, even name brands if you choose, for less. Of course, you have to **be willing** to buy used or "generic" goods; particularly when it makes good dollars and sense/cents. You can pay a third less for clothing, shoes, home goods, and more that results in an increase in significant amounts of dollars to pay down debt, save, and/or invest. I stumbled into a garage sale where everything in the lot was being sold for a dollar, including my vintage gorgeous handbag by a pricey, well known fashion designer. I also bought a cute little five-dollar dress and decided to research the label when I got home. To my great delight I discovered it was by another popular fashion designer I'd just come to know and its retail price was way more than I would ever choose to pay in a department store. I used my six dollars very well that day! I recently purchased a designer suit for $25.00 that would have cost upwards of four hundred dollars in a fancy mall store. When I wear my $1.00 designer bag, or $5.00 stylish boots, and $25.00 major designer suit for a fun day in a "fufu" part of town, I get compliments all the time and no one ever has to know what the items cost. I share these shopping adventures because I want to convince you that the extra money you pay for retail items or brand names does not necessarily yield "better"—better style, better fit, or better comfort. But shopping this way can yield a better bank balance reflective of less debt and more savings and lots of compliments.

Additionally, shopping this way speaks to a life of abundance and not deprivation. It is also just as much fun as buying retail; in fact, I find the "hunt" even more fun. Besides, buying resale is "green." Contrary to conventional financial wisdom, I am not a fan of living a life where you go without the things you enjoy most. Lack is not fun; nor is it a sign of abundant living. As you get to know me, you will realize another important goal of mine is to have lots of FUN on my current income. You may justify paying full price for retail items and brand names by saying to yourself, "Buying vintage is low brow, I want brand new regardless of the cost." But that is the emotional over-spender talking! Whether your income is $1,000 or $100,000 per month, the mindset and results of overspending are the same. If we spend more than we make, we will end up with debt weight. There will be times when you may find paying market value worth it. I do too at times, but those moments are rare. It's rare for billionaire and owner of Ikea who still shops at flea markets, according to an article by Billionaire New Worth. It's rare for Wall Street as well.

Again, greater financial success is not just about the amount of money you have right now, but how you manage the money you have right now. **From here on, you will manage that one dollar bill as carefully as you would manage a hundred dollar bill or a check for a million dollars**. I know for sure we must prove first that we can be grateful for and faithful with "little oil" and then increase will come. Living below your means is wise regardless of income. Buying low so you can live high means you begin shifting your spending priorities away from making full price purchases to a more strategic spending pattern of utilizing your money as a tool. It is the way to advance your long term CEO life vision, your life passion, or your personal wealth building activities. Just take a quick look at the phone book or google for online lists of thrift stores, consignment shops, swap meets in your area and give one a try. I bet you will really be surprised what great things are available and how much fun this kind of shopping can be. And remember, you don't have to tell anyone where you shop!

GATE FIVE: Money is Your Tool, Not Your Goal.

Money is a tool, much like a hammer and some nails. It is the "oil" or substance needed to create and implement a long term plan for building wealth for financial freedom, memorable life experiences, and to help others. I have always respected one dollar the same as a hundred. Coins or small amounts of money should never be seen as "pin money," "chicken feed," "mad money," "chump change" or "petty cash." There is no such thing. Thrown away pennies, nickels or dimes give the impression that there is disrespect for "smallness"—small money and small beginnings. This attitude, in most cases will stunt your financial growth or if you have a talent where someone pays you millions of dollars; you could very well lose it or be so poor in spirit you may still be miserable. Miserable with millions is not my idea of true wealth either. Let's view our income, no matter how little right now, as "wealth building blocks." It is what you have to work with to build a more secure financial future. Be clear that YOUR SELF-WORTH is never determined by how many or how few dollars you possess. This belief or feeling could very well be the cornerstone of real wealth building as well as the "cure" or way to less emotional over-spending.

With this core understanding in mind, I will now share how I used a small money tool and wielded it to build a very financially stable and secure wealthy life. How did I use my money as a tool as I was getting my financial life squared away years ago? Here is the story of my first real estate purchase. Right after college, like most people, I set forth into the big world with no savings, no connections, and no financial support and with the exception of my Big Mama's inspiration, very little guidance. My brother's description sums up my early years in a nutshell, "You stayed down to come up." Translating for my brother, I can say I chose to live below my means for a calculated period of time to build slowly but surely toward a stable financial state that would allow me to live healthy, wealthy and a lifestyle I love.

I lived in a tiny studio (400 square feet) apartment in South Central Los Angeles where my living expenses afforded me the opportunity to save a significant portion of my salary to later invest. I can't go into as much detail here, but there are a number of ways one can reduce housing costs, a major expense, to increase cash flow. I resisted family and peer pressure to move to fancy apartments, drive fancy cars, and wear "bling", though I could've easily afforded these things. It's so funny how living in "little houses" is so popular and trendy today, especially in big cities, like Los Angeles, New York. (It is also my second most effective wealth creation tool.) However, I did live my passion and travel below market value and still experienced the best of what each country offered on every continent, except Antarctica. I speak at length about this topic and more in my videos posted on the website.

After amassing well over many thousands of dollars, I needed for a down payment and just as the neighborhood was changing-- for my betterment I knew it was time to move. I saw a property that seemed to have great value, perhaps my dream house. I, a single woman with a small income called an agent and she arranged for me to see that place and several others. As we were driving, I began to doubt myself, to focus on my lack of resources, to question whether I could afford or was even worthy enough to live in such a nice neighborhood, to worry that I was wasting this nice person's time. I am so glad the Holy Spirit prompted me to remain quiet. Had I spoken about my fears, doubts, and distrust of my own abilities, I might have missed out on my first big step into my wealth building process. We all know that one does not wield hammer and nails with emotion. Money is just a tool you use in the same way as the hammer tool. One employs a hammer with specific direction and controlled force, addressing a precise target, the head of the nail. Likewise, we do not direct our dollars with our feelings, certainly not those of fear, doubt, and insecurity. Using my dollars emotionally that day, I would have missed out on the deal of a lifetime and perhaps never accomplished the life of wealth and abundance I have come to know since.

It turned out that my new mortgage payment was not significantly more than the rent I had been paying. For a couple hundred dollars more each month, I doubled my living space and decreased my drive time to work in Beverly Hills from thirty minutes to seven minutes. My new house ended up saving me both precious time and even gas money. I still own that property and remember fondly all the enjoyment I got from its big bay windows, its lovely green yard and peaceful surroundings. I also get great enjoyment knowing how I followed the advice of Wall Street shared earlier, buy low, sell high. I bought that property below market value and can now sell it for ten times more. This purchase marks the beginning of my very profitable career as a real estate investor. I have bought several properties since then and am on the verge of buying more in what they call a sluggish economy. I encourage you to find your niche and prosper. (By the way, the financial tips I share are all from my life experience and they have been proven to work in all "economies.") Think of how you can alter your living arrangements to acquire your "seed money." You do not have to live in a tiny apartment, though minimalist or small house living is becoming trendy in many big cities. There are a number of ways to go about this and I invite you to check out my videos where I go into more detail about this and other wealth building topics. Remember, the financial tips I share are only the ones I have used, so I can say they have worked for me and I believe they will work for you -- all of us working people who want to live like a millionaire on our budget.

GATE SIX: Don't Work For Your Money; Make Your Money Work for You.

What does it really mean to make your money work for you? Let's continue to delve into strategies with which you can build a lifetime of wealth and well-being on a solid foundation of stability by entering the gates we offer here. Here we are focusing on the short run, using what we actually have to work with right now. As you have probably already gathered, when I started my financial life, I was willing to take on an additional part time job, teaching in the evening. I lived strategically, saving for many years and I resisted getting into debt, even for my college education. I took out minimum student loans and did not fall into the trap of getting a credit card without having a stable income.

I live below my means and am always positioning myself to save 20 to 30% of my monthly income and keep my living expenses low, so I can afford to save and invest. Even today, I live on 65 to 70 percent of what I make, which gives me a great deal of wiggle room to not only save and invest, but make my money work for me so I can live the life of my dreams. There are ways you can take similar action to stretch your current income to make your money work for you. Ways like this require some strategic, creative, and out-of-the-box thinking. Think of ways you can reduce your living expenses, which usually costs a minimum of one-third of your take home salary, a huge chunk of your take home pay. Think of creative ways to maintain your current lifestyle, but for less. Think of ways you can reduce the cost of items you use every day. Do you have to have the best of everything right now? Let's get our financial house in order first and then the best will come. One of the most creative and effective ways to make your money work for you is based on the aforementioned concept.

I call it the **wait strategy.** Let's look at how we use or could consider using this approach in general, taking credit cards as an example. For example, if I charge something, I only do so if I am sure I can pay for it in full at the end of the month. If I am unable to pay at the end of the month, then that means I have to go without it for now, not forever. I am not a financial martyr! It may sound difficult, but it's easier than we think. New paradigm building. I can't think of anything I have wanted or any experience I have desired that I have actually gone without. However, over the years I have made conscious decisions to **wait** to purchase a designer dress or a new car when delay was necessary to achieve a bigger financial goal. **When I had a written, posted plan, I did my utmost to stick to it**. My friends have been known to say I am more disciplined than anyone they have ever met. I chuckle. I think I am just financially far-sighted. Of course, I still have a good time. Major purchases have to fall in line with my written plan. With my master plan in place, I travel the world, go to concerts and great parties. I enjoy life to the fullest. All the while I am saving and strategizing for the life I live and the next stage in life. What is your financial plan to make your money work for you? **Pause here and write about it**.

With my first real estate purchase I increased my living space, moved to the best location possible, acquired a gracious lifestyle, and still I continue to invest in property that appreciates in value, regardless of the vagaries of the rest of the American economy. My investment properties yield a profitable passive income, without the "headaches" people often associate with rental properties and tenants, a practice and passion that require just "a mother's wit". My study of economic history reveals to me that real estate investment is one of the best ways for an individual to build wealth, no matter the condition of the economy as a whole. If prices drop, they are sure to rise again, and again, and again. My mother always said to me growing up, "They are not making any more land." You've got to know where and how to buy. Location. Location. Location. It is the preferred method of wealth building for me, and it is how I've used the money tool to create financial success.

Can you think of ways to use your money tool to create the life you'll love? Can you reshape your financial life so that you stop living on more than you make? Can you spend significantly less than you make? **Yes, I believe we all can when driven by purpose.** Only that difference between the dollars you make and the dollars you spend each month is what you have to build your financial future. Those dollars are the only dollars you can use to hammer out a new life for yourself in the next five years, the next fifteen years, and the next fifty years. I call them *the purposeful dollars*. And they are enough! You've got to think out both short term and long term goals and write a vision of your own life and future abundance now. Become clearly focused on that and driven to achieve it. Your money habits will bend, change, and follow your new vision, your new purpose. That's how I have made my money work for me. Email me your plan to make your money work for you.

GATE SEVEN: Buy Necessities or Experiences, Not Objects.

How many times have you said "I am going to buy this item because it's such a great deal or because it's an amazing 80% off?" How many times did such a bargain "pay off" for you by really being useful? I cannot tell you how many times I have gone shopping with family and friends and bought nothing! It is OK. Sometimes, I stick out like a sore thumb, and other times, they marvel and compliment my discipline. In contrast, I have also watched them spend hundreds of dollars on stuff just because it was cheap or on sale. Yet long afterward the stuff still sits in the box untouched and unused. The items ranged from a cup to a comb, shoes to shirts, and a ring to other bling, almost anything just because it was inexpensive or cheap. This kind of spending is "expending," merely exhausting your resources pointlessly and dissipating your financial energy. Give yourself credit! That is, give yourself credit for being powerful enough not to live on credit cards as an over-spender. Watch out! I have found that emotional overspending tends to be contagious. If you go out with a friend who is splurging wildly, you may find yourself following suit in spite of your best intentions.

Another surprising dimension of overspending struck me when I went to a friend's house where she offered us a party atmosphere, where she gave us all gifts of the expensive garments and accessories she had purchased but seldom, if ever used. At first I thought "How generous!" and went home with my loot. The third time she did this, however, I began to feel guilty. It dawned on me that by accepting her discards I was becoming an enabler of sorts. I was supporting her pattern of overspending and frittering away her income. I never told her why I stopped coming to her give-away parties and I feel badly about that. But my conscience and my money consciousness tell me that I did the right thing. Her giving may be driven by a sense of emotional lack and my receiving made me feel like a poor orphan friend. I have learned such "deals" are not always "ideal" parts of our financial lives or our friendships.

Over the years I have also learned that I must first spend on the necessities of my life, food, housing, transportation, utilities, and that precious cell phone! After those things are taken care of, my spending is discretionary. Instead of buying stuff, I have learned I get a lot more value from buying experiences that I will remember and cherish my entire life, rather than more "stuff" I have to dust. Purchasing a grand day at the Louvre museum with a friend is a true joy and a permanent memory. A special twenty one day vacation tour of Europe is one of my most valued investments! Travel is my great life passion. Every trip I have ever invested in has been a transformational experience that still gives me enormous pleasure every time I think about it. No dress or car I ever bought has given me so much pleasure or resulted in making me a more cosmopolitan and worldly wise person. The friendships I have made, the walk up the Eiffel Tower, the debate about who invented flan in Argentina, personal tour following in the footsteps of U2, while discovering my own familial roots in Dublin, setting foot for the first time on North Africa, are just a few of my priceless experiences. Travel remains my greatest love, and I can't imagine any purchase more valuable to me. How is it done? All on a modest income, below market value, and an intense focus on what is really important, what matters most. Money always follows this kind of focus and passion.

What is it you love most? What brings you great joy? Perhaps your passion is a hobby like painting. Investing in all the materials and training and many hours associated with becoming more proficient in that activity may be the most worthwhile way of using the money and time in your life. I call this a transformational purchase, a purchase that truly makes your life richer. There will be moments where you splurge. Just remember when you indulge in overspending in your future, do so consciously and spend strategically on transformational purchases and experiences that improve the quality of your existence not just for the day, but for the rest of your life.

GATE EIGHT: Deprivation Is NOT Abundant Living!

In most books on money management, delayed gratification and personal sacrifice have been standard recommendations for one's financial success. With good reason such advice is likely to be dreaded and/or avoided by anyone seeking to have fun on his or her journey to a better financial state. To us "delayed gratification" means I can have what I want, maybe not right now. And "personal sacrifice" means I have to give up getting what I want entirely. Who wants to hear that? Who wants to live that way? Not me! Not I! Not you! But I can't honestly tell you that you can have everything you want right this minute either. **It takes time to repair financial damages.** What I do recommend is that you begin a life of conscious choices to limit self-destructive acts of spending excess by taking an honest look at your income and creating a plan to get out of debt. Decrease spending.

In our workshops, we share 40+ strategic spending tips to reframe our spending practices. **You give yourself an immediate raise when you spend less**. To not overspend right now is not the same as to sacrifice right now. When you think about "delayed gratification," I would like you to put the emphasis on the word "delayed." Why? Because to merely delay purchase means you are choosing to invest some TIME in strengthening yourself and your own financial health. Remember, time is money too. You are choosing to think "slow" about your money, to deliberate and consider the appropriate moment to purchase. **You do not forfeit the purchase; you forfeit only the emotional and impulsive component of the purchase**. I remember being at an event where a big ticket item was being offered for sale and there was a lot of pressure to buy now or miss the deal. I took time to think and say "Sorry, no." My friends, I know now that's the time to run, not walk, away. Strangely enough, I got a call a week later from that same salesperson offering the same "deal." What surprised me most was that I had completely forgotten about the item I once felt I really wanted to have. If this had actually been a meaningful purchase, then going without it could be seen as deprivation. As it was, I feel I had a narrow escape from behaving like an emotional over-spender paying for something I didn't really want.

We have to explore further to make clear distinctions. Financial life is not an all or nothing affair. We have been taught that to deprive ourselves altogether may be thought of as admirable or stoic or good for us in the long run. Nope. In my experience I find "slow" spending works best. Instead of choosing between overspending or deprivation, all or nothing, I engage in a review of and perhaps some modification of my budget to see if this purchase could be made in lieu of another or paid for by working a few additional hours. Would it be reasonable to purchase it after saving for six months? Deprivation means going without completely. Deprivation is choosing to deny yourself things that bring you pleasure, a direct contradiction of my basic idea of an abundant life.

Abundant living, as I loosely define it, means having enough money to live a fun, contented, and purpose filled life. That's hard if you are always saying "no" to the things that have meaning and bring internal satisfaction. Again, there is a definite place for delayed gratification; a time when you simply have to wait. Deciphering this is where the strategy comes in. But, and this is a BIG BUT, if this item is something you truly value and you are convinced it will provide you with a meaningful experience **that will last a lifetime**, not a mere moment of pleasure, you should consider, ponder the costs, and get it after some "slow" thinking, a budget analysis and a review of your practices of wise financial stewardship, and how it will impact your short and/or long term financial goals. This statement means, the final answer comes after you have considered all the costs, including the effect of the purchase on lifestyle, on your financial plan and family, friends, etc.

Let me give you an example of what such a moment looked like in my own life. I have always wanted a Diane Von Furstenberg wrap dress. I knew the original retail price of the designer dress and I learned where I could get it below market value. Even with that, it would still cost a pretty penny. Given our paradigm shifts, we know every penny matters because we are always on a master plan and the concomitant budget, even as our income grows and we decrease or eliminate debt. Therefore a splurge like this, even at a discount, could be costly because it would delay my financial plan. I reviewed my financial plan and decided the purchase would delay my rapid debt smashing campaign by several months, as a result of divorce. So when I wanted to make an impulsive decision and buy the dress anyway, I gave it some serious "slow" thought and eventually declined.

Now, my desire and goal is still to get a DVF wrap dress. Was I deprived? Hardly. I had plenty of beautiful clothes, and I still had a "dream." Fast forward a year to the day a colleague had a sale on high end fashions at her house. I wound up getting a DVF wrap dress for a price that literally had me jumping up and shouting "Hallelujah!" It had to be a DVF wrap dress; no substitute was acceptable. Having a DVF wrap dress was more than an emotional impulse or momentary craving. For me, having it and wearing it is a meaningful achievement, adding to my idea of being a cosmopolitan woman. Hanging in my closet, it is not an object, it is an experience I cherish. It makes me smile every time I wear it. Here's the key. Ready for this? **I only need one. I am satisfied with just one**. I am out of credit card debt (from divorce) and could easily by another and another.

But I don't need or want to. That's the shift we are making! **One is often enough, especially when that one thing is significant and meaningful**. Guess what, there were other DVF blouses and dresses for sale at my colleague's house as well. I tried every DVF item on and chose to buy just the one wrap dress though a couple other items fit and looked perfect on me. Yes, I had to resist the urge to buy every other DVF item, even with all my finely honed money management skills. I am right there with you emotional spenders. I get it. It is so easy to get caught up in thinking we have to have more. That hole in our psyches can result in digging a great hole in our wallets. The dress has intrinsic value for me not as a necessity but as an especially rich and lasting personal experience. If you have a DVF dress equivalent or a "must have" item, dream or experience, then you too should have it. You can have everything you want, perhaps now or in a well-planned future.

Remember, we are growing out of the habit of spending money to satisfy fleeting emotional needs. **No object or service you buy is ever**

going to fill that hole in your heart. Having multiple designer dresses and bags do not make me more cosmopolitan, nor do they signal I have arrived or as my students say, "got it going on." The biggest secret to getting everything you want is to not want everything but enjoy everything you've already got. Gratitude for what you already have is graceful; also a wealth building tool. If you want something specific like a DVF dress fiercely enough, the right time and opportunity to get it will come. Correction, the time and opportunity will actually find you. I never told the friend who called me that I was in the market for a DVF dress. When you have a powerful dream or desire you can actually manifest it for yourself. The experience will come to you. Few people are as wealthy as Warren Buffet, and he tells us "People seeking riches never have enough. Wealth is a state of mind. Wealthy people always have enough."

Warren Buffet to my knowledge only has one house and shops infrequently. In fact I saw a picture of Warren Buffet, Bill Gates, and Steve Jobs, some of the richest men in the world wearing what looked like plain blue jeans. Again, I am not suggesting you go without, but perhaps understand that less can truly be more. It is quite possible to marry pleasure and financial stewardship. Not deprivation but strategic planning, knowledge of shopping cycles, and attraction are all elements of having a great life experience.

Go to New Fit World TV.com to find more information on shopping cycles, best time to purchase almost every item of which you can think.

GATE NINE: Price Is Not The Same As Value.

We tend to believe we have to pay big money for something or it is of poor quality and not worth having. On the other hand, if it's expensive we assume the quality of the product or service will be superb. Beliefs like this keep us financially hamstrung. Well, I would like to share an experience from my own personal life that debunks this belief. I have been in situations where I have paid top dollar for something and been quite disappointed and in some cases I have spent very little and discovered great quality and enormous long time value. I have also paid top dollar for an item and been pleased. Let me elaborate before getting to the actual story

I have in mind. Yesterday, a 15 year old student was looking at beautiful athletic shoes in the store. To my amazement I discovered they cost more than $150.00 for the pair! Would this pair of shoes allow him to run a four minute mile or dunk a basket in his next pick-up game? Would the price of the shoes ever offer him $150.00 worth of true value in his life? How many hours would his parent work to pay for those expensive athletic shoes? Asking these questions help you with "mindfulness" while shopping, like do I really want to work 20 hours to pay for this item. This explosive method of thinking helps us determine how meaningful or significant the purchase immediately. The following story will illuminate this Gate even more, as it is even more personal.

It is the story about a trip to the dentist office. My friend and I both went to see a dentist in the same week. I chose to use my HMO plan to cover teeth cleaning and my colleague chose to pay out of pocket for the same service, since she considered our HMO low brow and felt that it probably had dentists who were not as good as private dentists. I went in for a general cleaning and came back with a clean bill of health. During her general cleaning, she learned her tooth needed to be pulled. Still refusing to use an HMO plan, she decided to pay for the tooth pulling also out of pocket by the same dentist, again thinking the quality of service was better. There was no convincing her to use her HMO plan, though I tried, tried, tried. This decision did not turn out well. Her private dentist pulled the wrong or healthy tooth, while the damaged tooth remained as she paid out of pocket for this service. Her dentist offered to correct the problem by pulling the right tooth if she would pay the same rate. My friend would have paid to correct the botched procedure had I not insisted she pay no more. Stop paying him! Finally, she stopped and he corrected the botched procedure at no cost.

Do you think my friend received value by paying more? Did she receive more? Did she get what she paid for? I share this with you only to refute the myth that paying more for something makes it better or more valuable or you get what you pay for. Paying less doesn't make an item worse. Both are simply not true! Price is indeed just whatever you pay. It has very little to do with quality. Sometimes advertising or a brand name seem to promise us great things like better health, more beauty, a better tennis game or an easier time fixing dinner, but how often are such claims justified? Amount paid doesn't determine quality, endurance, effectiveness or any other dream come true. I would venture to say that the student's running minute per mile will be the same in a less expensive pair of athletic shoes. Price doesn't give a product value any more than winning a million dollars would make you a more valuable person! I know this statement is not consistent with what society tells us, but it's true. Research reveals that many wealthy people appear to know this and take pains to pay less for their products and services. Doing so may be one of the ways they stay wealthy! Just look to our friends on Wall Street's mantra again, "Buy Low, Sell High!"

GATE TEN: Money is Neither Good Nor Evil.

There is widespread belief that "Money is the root of all evil." In fact, many people believe that the Bible tells us so. This is a serious misconception that leads to a false view of our proper relationship to the money in our lives. Go to The Bible, 1 Timothy, 6:10, and see how misleading this belief is. The Bible uses words which make a world of difference to us: "For the **love** of money is the root of all evil." Money is not the problem. The Bible tells us that **our attitude** toward money, the <u>love</u> of money, is where problems arise. Take to heart the view that money is evil and you may feel justified in staying poor! The poor may feel self-righteous because they believe they have no "evil" in their lives! One might even feel subconsciously complacent about living in poverty or feel that ambition is also evil or even feel that one who has more money is less moral and upright.

This widely held misreading of The Bible's words damages everyone it touches. When we hold fast to thoughts like wealthy people are greedy, money corrupts, money does not make you happy, etc., then we are subconsciously suggesting the status quo is fine and, perhaps, accepting lack or "just enough" as a healthy way of life. **Money is a tool.** Money is no more evil than a hammer. Certainly, money can be used for good or evil purposes, as can a hammer, but it has no inherent moral nature. As a method of exchange created by a society, money has no human characteristics. It is often personified unconsciously and this way of thinking can lead us to feelings like money is evil, undesirable, or not worth having, certainly not in abundance. Since our unquestioned beliefs and our careless thoughts can be so very damaging to financial increase, we need to shift this way of thinking to free ourselves to take and continue to go on taking the next right action so true wealth can manifest.

Financial author and radio host, Dave Ramsey says "Money doesn't have morals. It doesn't make decisions on its own. It's not good or bad until we touch it." Be clear, then, that the means by which one acquires one's money may be good or evil, that is, your own actions may have a moral valance. Clearly, one can use one's money for good or evil ends in this world. I would take Ramsey's view still further, however, and say that our underlying <u>attitudes</u> toward money, unconscious or conscious, can lead directly to good or evil behaviors in getting and using money. What is the problem with **the LOVE of money**? Does one have to be rich to love money? I think not, not according to The Bible! Does one have to actually have money to wander into evil or negative behavior? You can be poor and love money too much and you may engage in unscrupulous behavior to get more. To have money in one's life is not inherently sinful. In fact, to have one's survival needs met and enough to be comfortable as well means that one is more likely to be able to live easily inside our social mores. A powerful unconscious view that to live in financial abundance is morally dangerous may keep some of us chained to a perpetual state of lack and deprivation.

This kind of unconscious allegiance to a state of LACK may be the equivalent of and as equally damaging as impulsive overspending to fill an emotional void. Being poor and proud may border on needlessly living out the false premises that money is a curse and that having less makes us more virtuous. The Agrarian Age and to some extent The Middle Age tended to equate poverty with an odd kind of humility and moral rectitude. That may be why we still use terms like "filthy rich" or "filthy lucre." We imply with this view that if you have no money, you have the benefit of not being morally "tainted" by money. In truth, poverty hardly benefits a person in any way, much less morally. Poor housing, poor health care, poor education, poor safety, poor food, poor jobs, is the plight of the poor all over our planet. If this is you, I recommend an immediate shift. Take some time to clarify your thoughts here. Journal. Write me immediately and let's make the shift together.

SOLUTIONS

GATE ELEVEN: Get Conscious, Organized, and Pay in Cash.

Admit that you are an emotional spender. Let's elaborate on this principle mentioned earlier. The first step to solving any problem is to recognize and acknowledge you have a problem. Only then can you find a solution. Do not beat yourself up about spending because we are encouraged to do so by advertisers, sometimes family and friends, as well as the global consumer society in which we live and breathe. We have learned to soothe our feelings by stuffing our lives with "stuff." As we have emphasized consistently throughout this book, the nature of our relationship to and views of money needs to become more conscious in order for us to change our behaviors in positive ways. We can easily be unconscious of the value of one small dollar in our life. Gather all the strategies you can find in this book to help you "raise your own consciousness" as you engage in money transactions.

I have two related imperatives I offer my students in my workshops. PAY FAST. BUY SLOW. We've discussed the value of investing extra TIME in any purchasing decisions. Impulse or "fast" purchasing is the source of a great many problems for today's consumers. The one place I do recommend you move quickly, however, is in paying your bills. I strongly recommend the "fast" practice I use. When a bill arrives in the mail, I open it immediately. I write the check immediately. I put it in the envelope, stamp it and take it out to my mailbox right then and there to ensure bills are paid early. PAID FAST. I have been paying my bills this way for years. As a result, I do not ever have to worry about misplacing the bill, mailing it after its due date or otherwise messing up my financial peace. If you are unable to pay immediately, be mindful of due date (write on envelope) and mail so that it still arrives by due date. I highly recommend auto-pay for mortgage and other long term payments to ensure payments are never late.

In contrast, as we've pointed out before, I invest a lot of time in assuring that my purchases are "slow." I make a serious effort to take consideration of any large purchase home with me, away from the energy of the store, away from the smiling salesman, away from friends who tell me, "Oh, you really deserve that!" I am absolutely positive that one of the most powerful ways in which you can limit overspending is to make a habit of that "cooling off" period. Go home and analyze your motives and weigh the consequences of such a purchase. If the purchase truly meets that life value test of true significance and satisfaction, go ahead.

Another way to "slow" purchases, especially smaller, everyday purchases like those gourmet coffees four times a day or that Happy Hour cocktail after work, is to challenge yourself to always use cash. To actually hold the dollars in your hand and see them depart in order to acquire a cardboard cup of liquid can be painful if you really pay attention. When you pay with cash, you may be more likely to see the impermanence or feel the "hit" of your purchased item immediately. You can feel its "true value" in your life more vividly than if you were using that credit card or phone app. The blank face of a bank card always seems to make a purchase feel effortless and without consequence, at least at that moment. We do not usually take the time to think consciously about the long term value of the transaction and what it may or may not contribute to our life. Stay aware that you are spending, however small the amount. It all adds up! Pay cash in order to actually see the dollars leaving your life permanently.

GATE TWELVE: Affirmations Make Transformations

One path to a more abundant life is to practice regular use of affirmations. I define affirmations as declarations of truths that are in the process of appearing. They haven't come to pass yet; they're on the way. An affirmation is a gift you offer yourself to quell doubt and unbelief and express appreciation for your life in its current state. In my life I find great power in words and thoughts. I believe you have the power to change your spending habits and financial practices in general by first speaking what you want into existence. Establish a connection in a quiet place within you to say and affirm what you want to overcome—the old practices of overspending and other undesired behaviors. Create new thoughts, new words, and repeat new actions until they become habit and a natural part of your everyday life. Affirmations spur action that lead to desired transformations. We've offered you suggestions to help you form new money habits such as "Take time," "Buy low," and "Pay cash." But one of the most important new habits you can introduce into your money life does not appear at first to involve money at all.

I strongly recommend you begin the practice of speaking to yourself positively, always positively, silently or aloud, even in jest until doing so becomes a habitual and permanent way of life. Perhaps, some of we emotional money managers are already aware of how much negative "self-talk" we engage inside of our own heads that stunts our personal growth and financial progress. Most of us are our own worst critics. So the first step toward a more peaceful financial life is to stop upbraiding yourself about money mistakes you have made or things you have not done and feel you should have done. Let this resource be reflective of a new start or new beginning with your life management at large, and money management in particular. Here is an example of an affirmation I speak aloud and reminisce regularly. I find it endlessly supportive. I simply say to myself "I am enough." Sometimes I add "I have enough." And when I am feeling pushed at work or by finishing this book, I tell myself "I do enough." To me these are powerful and positive truths that bring peace, joy, and abundance into every area of my life. In my financial workshops, I encourage my students to create vision boards with pictures and words of affirmation that express their heart's desires. Speak and affirm what you want in your life, not what you do not want!

REFLECT: Which GATE had the most profound impact on you? How will you use it and others (as needed) to increase financial success?

CHAPTER 7

SEVEN STEPS OF REAL FINANCIAL TRANSFORMATION

We will now focus on seven actions you can take to begin transformation of your money life into even more of an abundant form. I have distilled my experiences down to seven of the most basic and powerful starting actions which can help you on your path of living like a millionaire now. Why start with only seven? Certainly, there will be other strategies and later long term phases of your fortune's growth. Many of these later stages of growth will be covered in a good deal more detail in the workshops, speaking engagements, and retreats offered by New Fit World TV to accompany this introductory book. However, I would like to leave you with more concrete action steps that will help you correct basic problems and work toward a stable foundation for long-term financial growth. I like the symbolic significance of the number seven -7, the number of completion. Number -7 symbolizes a sweet fulfillment like your favorite song created by this same number; 7 notes on a musical scale. Reflect on the 7 colors in a rainbow, and the beauty and signs of success and "we made it" that often comes after massive, drenching rains and huge, emotional challenges of life.

I hope that I have weaved this image of financial success, peace of mind, and enjoyment into a tapestry of colors, cozy like Big Mama's quilt. I think about the warmth and ease in thinking it brings; the faith and encouragement to keep on pushing; another essential component to living the good life now. As we are getting ready to close, I want to leave you with 7 transformative principles I practice and find important to us working people who embrace this concept of Mind Over Money, How to Live like a Millionaire on YOUR Budget. For the first four actions, I propose returning to the four "Rs" of my philosophy of education: relationships, reading, wRiting and aRithmetic. These following seven actions need not be taken in the sequence presented here. If another order suits your situation better, begin with whichever of the seven transforming action feels most comfortable or most important at the moment.

Transforming Action One: Get a Money Magnet and/or a Mentor.

"People Who Need People, Are the Luckiest People in the World"

Barbara Streisand, "People," lyric

The first "R" in transformation is relationships. Other people are continually working transformations on us, and we on them. In my life I have found that I am much more successful in accomplishing my goals when I work with and talk to someone else who regularly holds me accountable for my goals and actions; these acts generally keep me more focused. As you begin these actions in building your new financial state of well-being, I recommend that you recruit a trustworthy and caring friend or colleague or teacher, perhaps one who has established some financial well-being of his own already. Ask her to talk to you regularly as you work on the following transforming actions.

Perhaps begin by asking your friend to read these seven actions. Ask your friend, your new money mate, to give you feedback on how he feels you are doing in accomplishing your goals, not always but sometimes offering you his own advice. One of my mother's favorite sayings is "A problem shared is a problem halved." If you feel uncomfortable or embarrassed discussing your current financial successes or messes with a friend or colleague, I recommend you seek out the privacy of a local Consumer Credit Counseling Agency, if "messes" warrant. Consumer Credit operates as a free consumer support program. Although the representative will probably have specific tasks and goals she recommends, her advice is confidential and professional and should lead to better circumstances in relatively short order.

I believe it is imperative to get at least one other person directly involved in your growth process. We all need "people!" As I've mentioned earlier, I have had the distinct advantage of having wise money managers in my immediate family. My Biggie and Big Mama did not have the benefit of high school or college educations, but their credit scores have always been outstandingly high. Both own property and contribute in significant ways to their communities. My Biggie actually has a street named after her in her hometown. My father also was a teacher/district administrator all his life and he has always been a great role model of frugality, sensible spending, and simple financial wisdom that could easily be overlooked, but still relevant even by today's standards: turning lights off, keeping temperature at a specific setting, having a good work ethic, in addition to saving regularly, budgeting and living a disciplined life. My mother and high school English teacher and school Basketball Coach were instrumental in convincing me that I could compete and graduate from UCLA, and their help was invaluable in my getting my B.A. In fact, my first editor is called Mama. I have been very blessed with people in my life who have encouraged and guided me into the successes I have achieved thus far, including bankers, good real estate agents, pastors, and others. But one can never have too many helpers.

> I remember Bill Wither's wonderful 1972 song, "Lean on Me." You just call on me brother, when you need a hand. We all need somebody to lean on. I just might have a problem that you understand. We all need somebody to lean on.

Another way in which you can incorporate people into your wealth building process is to find an inspiring mentor who has himself realized big, big dreams; maybe dreams similar to yours that you may not know or have any relationship. I have "mentors in my head" who have inspired me through their music, business savvy, sportsmanship, and communication skill via television and social media. Bono, Richard Branson, Magic Johnson, Warren Buffett, Steve Harvey, Serena Williams, Wendy Williams, Elizabeth Warren, and Oprah Winfrey are just a few of these mentors. Thanks to the magic of the World Wide Web, we can study the brand of our heroes and "sheroes" to get a glimpse into their career and financial lives, and more. While I am a big fan of what they do, I am an even a bigger fan of their "who"! Who are they? Who and what motivates them? Who influenced and cheered them on their rise to the top? Who helps them manage it all? I get encouraged and learn when I hear how they've managed success and overcome challenges. Especially important when we are feeling fragile or frightened as we go through various stages of our financial development. Hearing their words of determination under adversity, how they remain at the top of their game, and how they give back is inspiring.

They have indirectly taught me different lessons about money matters, money management, money-acquisition, giving, and integrating financial success and "life" success at changing levels through anecdotal stories, interviews, and self-initiated research. In addition to this research, I daily read and study a wide range of related business topics to expand my heuristic knowledge and increase my productivity for at least 30 to 60 minutes per day. Though they all work in different fields, what I admire about all of them in addition to their talent is their heartfelt passion to give and help others by way of causes dear to their heart. Giving back to charities or causes that help others is not only for celebrities, but for us as well. We, too, can also be mentors to others.

I also owe much gratitude to ministries of various faith leaders who have shaped my wealth building principles by way of the Bible, specifically the "Tithe." One of the biggest of all investment tools is the Tithe, the practice of giving 10% of all earnings to a religious institution or charity of your choice, based on your preference. Regardless of your religious faith, or no religious practice at all, principles (financial laws), similar to gravity, "scientific" in a sense work for all. If you plant (invest) a seed or financial gift in the right soil, it will grow. I go into more depth about this principle, practice and how it actually works in my teaching sessions. For non-Bible believers, many years ago, I heard an agnostic Oprah guest say that he actually tithes and has received huge financial benefits from the seed sown, though he claimed no religious affiliation.

Oil tycoon, successful businessman John D. Rockefeller's quote echoes my belief though I haven't made millions **yet.** Rockefeller said, "I never would have been able to tithe the first million dollars I ever made if I had not tithed my first salary, which was $1.50 per week." This practice, tithing is the "insider secret" for my good and rising financial success. It is definitely a religious practice, but also considered an investment strategy to many business and religious leaders. It is the wealth building strategy I have been practicing all of my adult, working life. I guess you can call this my business training as I learned tithing from my grandmothers' example. These beautiful women have served as walking examples of faith in action and personal mentors, people who have served as teachers and role models for me.

I say this to encourage you to build relationships with a wide range of people, from all walks of life. Forge relationships with your banker, a successful business leader or money manager, teacher and ask them to hold you accountable for your "homework", as heuristic knowledge (insider information) is shared. In addition, keep in mind there is someone out there who needs your insight, your support, and your mentorship. Consider the words of founder/CEO of Virgin Richard Branson, as it conveys the message succinctly "When I am asked, what is the difference between a promising businessperson and a successful one, mentoring comes to mind. Giving people advice on how they can best achieve their goals is something that is often overlooked."

As CEO of our household and lives, I hope I have convinced you that we are all business persons in need of mentorship. Tap into the words of great minds like these and people you admire to find out more details about their financial habits and lifestyle in general beyond just their celebrity or wealth. Ask them how they achieved their purpose. You may just receive an answer. This is the reason I created Net Fit World TV. It is a point of access for you to other people all over the world and for us to share with people all over the world. Fellow seed-planters share their experiences, rainy days, happy days as we journey on together. I invite you to join the New Fit community where we will work as a team on Saving Challenges, explore creative ways to shop, cook, sightsee, and have fun in our hometown, etc.; all over the world at affordable and even FREE prices. I can't wait to share more with you and learn from you when you reach out to me in our online financial fitness community at NewFitWorldTV.com.

Transforming Action Two: Know Thyself!

We have emphasized from the beginning how important it is to become more conscious of the beliefs which underlie our thoughts and actions, and we have illustrated how necessary it is to modify beliefs that hold us back and undermine our efforts to grow financially. For example, the mere belief that you live in LACK can be a self-fulfilling prophecy. Shift! Believe in abundance and move toward a life of abundance. So identify sabotaging beliefs and thoughts and modify them in order to move forward. The ancient maxim "KNOW THYSELF" means many things in different contexts, but for us it means we must pay careful attention to our beliefs and thoughts about getting and spending our money. The second "R" and the second transforming action is to READ OURSELVES well. We examine and consciously "shift" our paradigms where appropriate and stay clearly connected to our basic beliefs. You must know your own thoughts where you are, and what you want in your money life.

In practical terms, **Know Thyself** also means that we must begin transformation by <u>**assessing**</u> **exactly where we are right now financially**. This will require that we take a very detailed and perhaps painful look at our current income and our expenditures and our savings and our debt. If we don't know where the starting line is, we can't be in position for the race. A good pencil and four sheets of notebook paper are the basic tools to start with. On the first sheet of paper identify as precisely as possible **all your sources of income**. First and largest for most of us is our salary for employment. If you work on a commission basis or in a position in which you earn tips as well, you may need to average your monthly income for the last twelve months or so to arrive at a single monthly base salary. Or if you are self-employed and your income varies, add your monthly expenses to determine a rough estimate of the amount of money you need to make annually. Average your disposable income. You may have additional sources of income such as alimony, child support, part time work, regular gifts from relatives or regular interest income on savings. For now, omit occasional or temporary sources of income like baby sitting or hobbies or stock market increases. Your tax preparation forms for the previous few years may provide a quick overview of your regular income sources over time.

The second sheet of paper you create for yourself must be a picture of your **necessary regular monthly expenses**, as precise as you can make it. What is your rent or mortgage? If you own your home, what of costs for maintenance, insurance, gardening, security, in the course of the last year? What is the average monthly cost for these aspects of your living space? What are average monthly costs for your home utilities and internet, wireless and cell phone services? What is your average cost for gas for your car or cost for bus or train passes to get to work? What are other costs associated with your transportation to and from work? Auto insurances, including AAA, repairs, and car washes all count as transportation costs. If you have paid for groceries with one credit card or with checks only, you will have a paper record which will allow you to estimate pretty accurately how much you spend monthly on food store purchases. These things—shelter, utilities, transportation, and food—will likely constitute your monthly "**NEEDS**."

On a third sheet, go on to estimate **your expenditures on "WANTS."** How much do you spend during an average month on dining out, from cafeteria lunches at work to that big date on Valentine's Day and the outrageously expensive movie popcorn on Saturday nights? What do you estimate you spend each month on other "wants," perhaps those emotional overspending purchases we have discussed? Include sports games, concert entertainments, tobacco, alcohol, clothes, haircuts, manicures, spas, gyms, personal trainers and so on, things that might not be necessities. Of course, we will soon take great care to put the monthly income total sheet next to the average monthly expenditures total sheet for both needs and wants to see if you are currently running your own life business in the red or the black.

On your fourth sheet of paper, write down any **unexpected or particularly large expenses** which occurred in the last year. These expenses might include medical or dental bills, a major car or home purchase or repair, a vacation, a tax liability from last year. Large one time purchases like a television, computer, cell phone, and calling plan can be listed to highlight capital investments you've made. These may also be long term charges on your credit cards which could constitute a long term indebtedness you will need to take into account in your future planning. So the third "R" in our transformation is "aRithmetic." Do the math here.

Compare your income and your expenditures and see your bottom line. You may go to New Fit World TV for free download of these tracking documents or even online to mint.com if you prefer not to do it by hand. I believe doing it by hand to be the more powerful method.

"To thy own self be true." These famous words from Polonius in Shakespeare's classic <u>Hamlet</u> are often dismissed as a worn out adage spoken by a dithering old man. On the contrary, I think these words have great power for us in our financial lives. If you cannot tell yourself the truth, how will you ever grow in financial truth and increase? If you don't put yourself first, you will always end up, at best, second, struggling to make ends meet. If you do not follow your own vision, whose life will you be leading? One aspect of your future will be building a budget and a savings experience into your life. This is the fourth "R," "wRiting." Perhaps think of it as "Righting" your financial future by wRiting your strategic plan.

**Go to NewFitWorldTV.com to print easy to complete budget and financial tracking worksheets.

Transforming Action Three: Radical Thrift, No More Drift.

Once you have established with your "aRithmetic" and "wRiting" what your "financial state" is like currently and what you wish it were like, you can begin to take actions to restore it to stability and begin to live a more balanced money life, a life on an "even keel." If your four assessment sheets reveal that your financial state has been running in the red, with income regularly less than expenditures, then some belt tightening in your lifestyle is going to be called for, at least for a while. What does it mean to call a program of thrift "radical?" Well, the word has many resonances which are applicable here. Radical is used in fashion news such as the term "radical chic," meaning new and cutting edge work by a designer; in this case the designer is you. The kind of thrift I term "radical" here is also fundamental and thorough. I am calling for a program of thrift which goes to the very "root" of the problem. In short, I am calling you to genuine transformation. Be sure, thrift which is "radical" intends to re-form, to re-shape and to re-store your relationship to your own money.

Inherent in phrases like saving time, saving money, saving space, is the experience of reduction, decrease. If your financial state is running in the red, it is important to design and put into effect an intentional period of reduction of your indebtedness and a plan for conscious reduction in your expenditures. We have given you many in this resource to get started. Book and time restraints limit what more we can provide here, but our workshops, retreats, and seminars affords us more time to create a financial and life plan, while having fun in sunny southern California. We will also travel to you, no matter where you live. Reach out to us online for more information.

A monumental first step in radical thrift for some of us will be the reduction of long term existing debt. Assistance in consolidating debts if need be (last resort) and arranging a schedule of regular but manageable payments can be found through Consumer Credit Counseling Services. If you are willing to make the phone calls and negotiate lower interest rates or lower payments, you can do these things yourself. For many of us, though, the aversion to thinking and talking about our financial messes, is very powerful. Of course, while you are reducing your debt weight, it is crucial that you incur no new debt. Here is what I highly recommend, for starters. Get rid of all but one card for emergencies. Make sure your new card is fee free and interest free, and widely accepted. Forget frequent flier miles for now. Wonder, if your gas cards and retail store cards should be cut up to streamline your wallet. If you should experience a short term debt crisis now or in the future, be brave and call the Customer Service Representative or Manager of the creditor or the bank yourself. It is their JOB to help you resolve your problem promptly for your sake as well as theirs. I was very pleasantly surprised by how much cheerful assistance I got when I had a money flow problem when I first started teaching in a small private school.

To my horror, this new teacher discovered that her school had issued her a bad check in payment for her services! (I soon changed jobs.) As a responsible money manager I had already sent in the check for my car payment. Right away I called the finance company which held the loan on my car and told the Manager my sad tale. Alerted to the fact that he too was about to receive a bad check, and seeing that I had a consistent and timely paying record, he arranged that I got not a mere one month extension on the due date of my payment, but he gave me a three month extension! (This was a big help in transitioning to a new job.) From this I learned that establishing a relationship with your creditors and relevant Customer Service Representatives can be a valuable part of your people support system. Obviously, I also learned never to write a check before the money is actually in the account; a practice still applicable in this age of auto pay. I also learned that if I had delayed facing that problem for even a few days, the problem would not have been resolved so quickly and so satisfactorily to my benefit. Act quickly when something goes awry. No more financial "drift." By that I mean **no longer fritter away your dollars.**

Unconscious and Emotional Overspending must decrease, if not come to a complete end, clearly, as part of your radical thrift program. When you feel impelled to purchase something, even something as seemingly trivial as a $5.00 Latte Macchiato, to cheer yourself up or to celebrate a moment of triumph, give yourself the gift of TIME instead. I am a coffee lover. Spending fifty dollars a week in coffeehouses on the way to work and back was a wonderful luxury I was sure I deserved. But eventually I got practical and bought a nice pot for my office and some lovely coffee Arabica beans and began making my own treats. I am the richer and thinner for it! We have pointed out that if you delay an impulse purchase, the impulse will usually go away, if not then find cheaper, alternative ways to acquire it. This choice to delay a purchase or find a less expensive alternative can be the very heart of your new savings program.

When I want something, I wait a few days at least to cool down and deliberate about why I desire it and how worthwhile the purchase. I consider how many hours of work is needed to pay for the item. After due deliberation in my current solid state of financial well-being, I can choose to go ahead and purchase that object if I want it or need it enough. You too will be able to do this later when you are running in the black. (Paying cash also empowers you to do this now.) Right now, radical reduction of debt and expenditures is the goal, so it is best to abstain from purchases, even small ones for a while. You are in thrift training. Seek Transformation!

Transforming Action Four: Plant and Grow your new life.

Like mustard seeds, the seeds of abundance are tiny. Do you know someone who throws away pennies? I would never toss away a penny, even in a wishing well! Well, occasionally I do, in a romantic moment. But more often, I am bewildered when I see pennies, nickels, dimes, and now sometimes quarters tossed onto the street. I truly believe "A penny saved is a penny earned." Does that make me "a penny pincher?" I stay in touch with the fact that every dollar I've ever had grew from one hundred small pennies. (Our saving challenges will begin with 1 cent.) I encourage you to become a "penny pincher" too. Pennies are like little seeds. In my financial life, I can plant the tiniest of seeds, a tiny seed of thrift, even a penny, in good soil, tend it well and it grows me a "dollar tree".

Here is that powerful metaphor of growth again, using the disciplines of tilling, planting, tending, and harvesting. We don't plant one seed usually: we plant many. Nature scatters many seeds and scatters them far and wide in order to create, preserve, and protect the new generation of growth. Here are some action seeds of abundance I have taken and continue to practice that I think will help you plant and grow your very own "dollar tree." I give you 40+ in the workshop, but will only provide you with a few here in the interest of time and maintaining your attention. Each one may seem small, but one seed of thrift can make a tree and many seeds of thrift make a harvest. Plant as many of these seeds of thrift as possible and watch your money tree grow. It is harvest time y'all (you all)!

One seed to your financial harvest might be to start your own bank, your own piggy bank, called the "bank of you" for now, in addition to your traditional bank account. Every night make it a habit to empty your wallet or pockets of all your change. Put it in a bowl or jug or piggy bank. Maybe with every penny, nickel, dime, or quarter you drop in, speak a word of affirmation and multiplication for your new financial habit. You will be surprised to find how quickly your change grows into hundreds of dollars. I know people who have taken vacations as a result of simply habitually saving their coins.

Waste not: want not. Four simple words that are easy to say and rather hard to do. But take a few minutes per day initially to go over your "needs" and your "wants" expenditure sheets from Transforming Action Two. Note or highlight where your dollars are going to waste. I was spending as much as $10.00 a day on lunch. I started taking my lunch to work and stopped buying potato chips and sweets, and both my budget and my waistline benefited. Gym membership? Either go to the gym or stop paying for it. I didn't give up my beloved and relaxing hair salon appointments, but I switched from every two weeks to every three weeks. Your costly habits may differ from mine, but identify them and shift. Consider the costs of expensive harmful habits like tobacco or alcohol or gambling which will obviously yield not only huge savings, but better health and decreased doctor visits and doctor bills.

Among your credit cards and bills are hidden fees, ignored interest charges or late fees from simple bad timing. Parking tickets, ATM charges for out-of-network transactions, currency conversion charges when you travel abroad, and expensive printed checks tend to result from simple neglect or inattention. Be conscious and save. Read any applications for cards or loans very carefully and refuse any with costs in small print. Invest a little bit of time and attention and you will find current money feels like a wage increase, debt decrease, and now you can make significant savings.

If you are unsure about something, communicate with a person who should be able to educate you. Use that I-phone! If a charge on any of your bills is a mistake, get it removed; if a charge is optional, remove it. If your contract for a service like your newspaper or television or phone service has just increased its cost, call and tell the company you wish to cancel because you can't afford or do not wish to pay this new price. True, right? Often, the Customer Service Representative, your financial friend, will offer you continued service for the former price or even some better special pricing. If he doesn't, you don't have to actually cancel, unless you think you can live without it. In most cases, they want to retain your business.

There are so many steps you can actually take right now (too many to name here), to rearrange and reallocate your current spending habits to help you achieve your financial goals. Remember, this is a thrift program to stabilize and begin to grow your wealth in your life. Utilizing the aforementioned suggestions alone can save you hundreds and perhaps even thousands annually after implementation. No reductions you make right now need to be permanent. Whether you are saving a penny from your pocket or saving hundreds on a new auto insurance policy, these seeds of thrift will grow slowly but surely into dollars that might have otherwise slipped through your fingers.

**Go to NewFitWorldTV.com to find information to help you shop more strategically on everyday items by knowing the best time to purchase almost every item you use daily, team saving challenges, and more.

Transforming Action Five: Have Fun!

Many of us are accustomed to spending lavishly on our entertainment and travel pleasures. We work hard and feel we deserve the best. I sometimes splurge myself, after a careful review of my budget and all necessities and bills paid. I do not believe in deprivation in my life and I like to have fun. All work and no play would make me a dull girl! I do not intend to make a living to the exclusion of making a life! I want the same for you. But even in this area of enjoyment, I find I need to make time to plant a seed of thrift so I can splurge wisely on occasion. Travel is my passion and depending on time of travel, I may pay full price for airfare and go to upscale spas for relaxation and rejuvenation.

Having fun and splurging do not need to be expensive however. Simple pleasures are also amazingly satisfying. Enjoy a twenty minute chat with a good friend at a coffee shop. A television show with your kids. A Sunday drive to the beach with your favorite person. My friends and I make a great game of finding the liveliest entertainments for free. All over many cities, especially in the summer, are free festivals, movies, poetry readings, concerts in the park, as well as tennis courts and soccer fields for play and lovely trails for scenic hikes. I occasionally splurge for an expensive concert with my beloved Beyonce, but I find games of Monopoly with my nephew, picnics and hikes, and solitary sunbaths give me a stream of additional joys in my life at no cost. For most people food and fun go together. Food is a major expense that we take too much for granted. We often waste a great deal of money in our eating behaviors estimating around $1,200 per person annually according to a 2014 survey.

Think of how cutting that waste in half can contribute to extra funds for you to deploy strategically toward your financial goals. What of the FUN factor? Most of our fun activities have food consumption built into them before, during or after. No one wants to live without celebrations and date nights and food explorations. I try to just limit the frequency of dining out in a variety of restaurants by scheduling my activities with care; for example I may forego my typical Sunday afternoon meal out if I am going to celebrate on Tuesday evening by treating my friend to a birthday dinner. There are some restaurants where one can take a friend where the birthday person meal is free or at a discount. Be sure you know your friend well, if you opt for this route. Even I the money magnet was not happy when a first date took me to dinner and paid with a coupon. If it's a milestone birthday or monumental occasion, I will splurge on my friend and myself at the best restaurant in town. Remember, we can marry financial responsibility and get some of our wants met. The most fun is really in the pleasure I find in my friends and family, not in the menu or how much I spend. Cooking for friends at home is also a preferred choice as there is joy in having people over laughing and talking and enjoying themselves around a table of food I prepared. I like to say, it's what's around the table, not what's on the table that matters most. In fun, food and money, moderation always serves us best.

Transforming Action Six: Financial Organization

While you are transitioning into financial stability, I recommend that you get in the habit of paying each bill as soon as you open it. As I have already stressed, "Pay Fast." Write the check; put the stamp on the envelope; put it in the mailbox ASAP to avoid late fees, increase FICO score, hone new habits, and maintain absolute conscious control. In this period of financial transition I find my students benefit from actually seeing and touching their statements; payments each month. Doing so builds one's consciousness of what one is paying for and exactly how much one is paying. A history of prompt payments established in this way will also raise your credit score so when you want to buy a new car or a house, lenders will welcome your arrival with a great big smile. I have a great credit history with a car company where I was never late or short on a payment, and when I decided to upgrade they gave me the car of my choice at the **price I named, without a credit check.**

Later, when you know you're financially organized, you may want to automate the process with direct deposit of your salary and online bill paying as I have with **select** payments. But for now I suggest you stay in touch with what is coming in and what is going out each month by utilizing the "snail method" of bill paying. When bill paying this way, remember that the money must be in the bank when you write the check and it must stay there until the payment is complete. Don't play "the juggle game." You cannot count on the mail being slow and the bank taking its time to process your check. In these days, both the U.S. mail and your bank are fully automated and your check is likely to move very quickly from your hand to theirs. Don't risk an overdraft. In fact, I usually keep an extra cushion of at least five hundred dollars in my checking account (whatever amount you can afford) because I have found that unusual circumstances like a four day holiday can foil my management efforts. The bank may be closed and not process my direct deposit at the usual time. When the bank reopens the next week, the checks I wrote during that interval can easily be processed by a machine somewhere well before my direct deposit is recorded. The result would be an unfortunate and unexpected overdraft, or two or three, if I did not have my little cushion in place. Even today with an overdraft protection account, they would charge a fee so I find it best to maintain the extra padding even while automating.

This is another reason that you might consider automating long term payments like mortgage, insurance, car payments, or student loans shortly after you balance your finances and become organized. And consider arranging all your due dates if possible so they fall around the same time of the month… a few days after the first of the month if the first is your regular pay day. But be cautious if you do automate your relationship to money and review accounts weekly so that you stay in touch or abreast of your actual financial state. A company might increase its charges without your noticing it or you just go on and on getting charged for a service you no longer use or value like movies online, a gym membership, cable stations you don't watch or a magazine you don't read anymore. You also should know if you choose to stop automated payments, the company has to agree to sever these ties. So I emphasize that, if you do choose to automate, you automate only your large and long term payments that are essentials in your life and monitor often. Here is a budget allocation plan I recommend to become financially stable and organized, modify as needed.

Budget Allocation

CHAPTER 8

WEALTH GENERATING GIFTS & TALENTS STEP

Transforming Action Seven: Begin Your Quest for Financial Success

"To attract money you must focus on wealth. It is impossible to bring more money into your life when you are noticing you do not have enough because that means you are thinking thoughts that you do not have enough." Rhonda Byrne, <u>The Secret</u>

We have been emphasizing throughout this book that aligning our feelings, thoughts, and actions is essential to managing and growing our money strategically. This alignment resembles what Byrne calls "The Secret." The importance of alignment is not new to us. Remember Napoleon Hill's "Think and Grow Rich." Proverbs 23:7 affirms the classic wisdom: "As a man thinks in his heart, so is he." Even in this resource, we began with the role of feelings, thoughts, and actions in connection to our money and how to use money as a tool to help us increase our financial success by doing the following strategically: save, budget, plan, and spend wisely; crucial elements of any financial transformation.

However, any work on financial abundance would be remiss if it did not address how to bring more money into your life so you simply have more "dinero" with which to work each month. I believe each of us can become what I call a money magnet and begin to generate his or her own field of attraction, pulling money in from every direction. We need to explore how to bring more money into your life NOW. There are many commonly cited ways to attract more money: strategic spending, extra jobs, hobbies, start a side business, investing in real estate or stocks and bonds, etc. In previous workshops I used to offer attendees lists of actions they could take to earn extra cash. I no longer offer such suggestions except upon request. I have come to see the path to additional income and overall work as much more specific than that. I believe that each person needs to identify his own purpose and vision. **The source of financial abundance is inside of you.** Your "secret" is something you are born with, something absolutely **unique** to you. Big Mama calls it your "BENT."

When I was growing up, I remember Big Mama would speak often about certain relatives in terms of their "bent." Cousin Leen was "bent" to sing. Aunt Tomp was "bent" to cook. Cousin Leen's grandson at only two years old could already be seen as "bent" to become a talented drummer. By the time Ty turned five, he was playing drums for our family's church. This feat is especially amazing because our church has very high standards for what we call a "joyful noise" every Sunday. Without training, Ty played so well he dazzled us all. Big Mama says he was "bent" to be a drummer. I heard this term "bent" so often when I was growing up, I thought it was actually in the Bible. After much research, I never did find the term.

However, one day I found a similar concept in Hebrew, called "hanak." "Hanak" refers to the unique personality trait of a child. This trait expresses the true essence of the child's self, his true gift deeply within. We are born with it. Following your "bent" in life leads to an authenticity that is a deeply admirable form of aligning feeling, thought, and action. Pursuing, expressing, and "gifting'" the world with your unique "bent" will open doors to all kinds of wealth and abundance. Opportunities far beyond your wildest dreams can appear. So instead of being content with cookie cutter to-do lists, go for generating your own special powers as a money magnet, emitting your own field of attraction, pulling financial resources to you from unique directions beyond what you can currently imagine or think. Can you see your own "bent?" Think back to elementary school, and reflect on your natural abilities at that time. Like Ty, I recall students who were naturally gifted in the area of gymnastics, the arts, and sport, though they'd never had any formal training. I believe this path is the "path" we should take and pursue. Can you imagine Picasso serving pizza?

Are you doing something that doesn't express your authentic self? If the answer is yes, that's OK. That is the case for many of us.

When I graduated from college, I took a series of odd jobs just to pay bills. Eventually, I began to work toward a profession that allowed me to express my "bent." I have always incorporated money lessons into my academic lessons. As a natural outgrowth of my classroom lessons, along the way, I have created my own business that allows me to teach in new ways to a whole world of new "pupils." Seeing clients' FICO scores increase is equal to the satisfaction I get when I see students grasp a new academic concept and increase their test scores. I continue to teach as I love it and it provides the financial foundation I need to pursue new outlets as a teacher/entrepreneur (teacherpreneur) with my communications company. One day, I affirm we will be the world's leading resource and "go to" company for all things needed to live like a millionaire on any budget.

The great Greek philosopher, Aristotle, said: "Where your talent and needs of the world cross, there lies your vocation." Whatever your "hanak", write, sing, speak, construct, drum, cook, preach, teach, run for mayor, or play ball as passionately as you can. Once you feel, think, and act into your own "bent", true transformation occurs. Desire for stuff decreases. Living according to your "bent" increases. Financial wealth increases. Peace of mind and focus of action increase. True wealth is when the wealth in you increases. Be patient. The fruit of a seed planted takes time to manifest. Richard Branson is fond of saying "It takes years to become an overnight success." In the process of discovering your "bent", you may have to continue your work on your daytime job or career, while working your "hanak" on the side for a while. Just know that you are on the right path when you shift your thinking from having a single income to multiple streams of income, the most secure wealth in terms of dollars and cents. I live by the belief that I would rather have one hundred people pay me one dollar, than one company pay me a hundred dollars.

As CEO of my own life, I had a work experience that confirmed the need for multiple sources of income. I was an employee in a supervisory role for eleven years. Though our program flourished and became the second most profitable one in the company under my leadership and my performance evaluations were excellent, a new unit leader demoted me to a lower ranking, taking away my supervisory duties. I believe he did this because I would not commit actions in violation of labor law and my integrity. I am sure this action was taken to retaliate and hurt me for coming to the realization that I made a decision that honored the status and reputation I spent years building. My supervisor's action, though painful, cemented a shift in my thinking from full-time employee to full-time employer and the kind of workplace environment I envision. My vision, your vision, our vision is coming into fruition.

I later that same day had dinner with my friend and Discover the Edge business owner, Nicole Jansen. She specializes in helping people create their own businesses. Nicole was a great inspiration for me. She said something so powerful that it moved me to quote her here, as it speaks to my lifelong practice and philosophical approach to the work place. Nicole said, "We are moving to the One-Person Corporation where people are realizing that whether they own a business, have a job, or neither they are their own corporation called 'You, Inc.'" I call myself a "teacher-preneur", a teacher with entrepreneurial activities that lead to multiple sources of income. Like we've discussed, we working people have to be quite resourceful these days to live the life of our dreams. Those benefits and retirement packages of the Industrial Age are no longer guaranteed to us in today's Information Age. Research states you have a 400% better chance of becoming a millionaire in your life if you start a business. If this is your desire, start preparing now. Keep your day job. All healthy financial growth takes time and your current income is your building block.

Successful ventures begin with a written vision, where you see yourself doing and being what you were born to do; you write the vision, you think, you speak, you express gratitude, and you take corresponding action until it manifests. I saw myself as a Real Estate Investor in my high school years, long before I bought a property. Michael Strahan saw himself as co-host of Kelly and Michael while Regis Philbin was still host. This great gift of speaking, writing, and believing in our bent may sound like a far-fetched paradigm shift, but it is a successful practice we can all implement in our lives; our student life, our careers, and our entrepreneurial pursuits. Many other factors too numerous to include in this one book contribute to financial abundance in your life. Other things like eating, exercising, socializing, marrying, and especially tithing can have a profound impact on attaining and maintaining financial success. Tithing, in fact, probably deserves an entire book itself. It is my number one investment strategy. Sir John Templeton of Franklin Templeton Investments says "Life's greatest investment is the tithe." Remember the story of the impoverished widow at the beginning of the book. She had only "two mites" (½ penny) to give to the treasury, but Jesus called her donation the greatest of all. It matters not the size of your salary, your vision, or even your home; small daily actions of investing in your financial goals will yield a financial return, some thirty, sixty, and even one hundred fold.

REFLECT: The number 7 represents completion. What role will your "bent" play in your financial transformation? Email me your answer.

CLOSING REMARKS

On your quest for financial success and wealth building think about the legacy you're creating. Legacy is often used to describe the property or assets people leave their heirs when they pass away. Let's expand our definition to include non-material assets as well. We also leave a "non-material" legacy behind: our family name, our family values, our relationships, and our lifetime achievements. A legacy of financial practices, money management skills, belief systems, and relationship-building with merchants, banks, community, and people of all nations and socio-economics is the richest asset Biggie and Big Mama gave me. Through their words and examples, they left me and other family members with a legacy, a way of life that yields inner wealth and financial success in any era.

Language, by way of the worldwide web and local community allows us to reach out to people, to connect, support, and grow organically as we touch one another with our passions, disappointments, successes, and innermost desires. Spoken words, affirmations, graceful gratitude is the true legacy we leave behind. They manifest themselves in how we think about money, how we acquire money, and what we do when we get money. It is customary to believe money and property is one's greatest legacy. However, the history of how we feel and interact with family is the legacy often left behind and expressed in how heirs manage their material inheritance. Non-material legacy or heritage trump the passing of material wealth alone. To strengthen your legacy for your heirs, ask yourself these questions.

Are you sharing the values that made you wealthy with your immediate and extended family, particularly your children? What kind of feelings about values, money, possessions in this life are you demonstrating to your family members, your colleagues, and majority of the people with whom you interact often? How do they feel when they leave your presence? Are you seeking riches for the sake of riches? Or are you pursuing your purpose, where material wealth is not the goal, but the byproduct? The answer to these questions is your legacy. Do you know that many people who have become billionaires didn't seek to be billionaires? For many billionaires their legacy is more important than their money, according to Martin Fridson, as quoted by Quenten Fottrell in an article in <u>Market Watch</u>. As they become older, Fridson states, many billionaires say "I never set out to be a billionaire; I set out to do good."[9] As we start our journey to increased wealth and making a great legacy, let's ask ourselves how can we do good? How can we help somebody? How can we pass on the values and traits that made us wealthy to our own family members? Both material and non-material wealth can be placed in your will, trust. And of course, as we leave our monetary wealth (no matter the amount), we are also wary that we are indeed leaving a legacy, which could also be defined as a great name! (And sometimes, it might just make us famous!)

I hope I have made you feel better about yourself and your achievements at this stage of your financial life as well as your prospects for future abundance. Though we have to deal with real problems and obstacles along the way and address some of the touchy, emotional stuff we encounter in our overspending on our quest for authenticity, you will find the result of great worth. I hope I have inspired you to pursue your passion and fulfill your purpose for living by using your money as a tool to build the life of your dreams. You really can live like a millionaire on your current budget by simply deciding **now** to do so. Use your money as your tool and get to work. Work on the emotions, thoughts and actions that seem appropriate for you as your starting place. It's just a matter of "mind over money."

True wealth is actually more than just money; it entails having more than enough to live the lifestyle you desire, though dollar amount varies per person. It is also quality relationships where you are emotionally fulfilled and connected. It is building and passing on family values, wisdom, and resources; particularly the wisdom of how your family achieved wealth. True wealth includes joy and laughter and good times with the people you love. Your smile, your idiosyncrasies, and quirky ways are also symbols of great wealth. Decrease the triggers and emotional spurs in your spending. Take transforming actions and begin construction of that mansion of abundance, move in and live like a millionaire for the rest of your life. I lovingly leave you with these affirmations:

May you be all you want to be and all you were born to be!

May you live your life on purpose, in emotional and outward prosperity!

May you have a new outlook that fuels and serves you well all your life!

May you continue to grow, learn, and live according to your true passion!

May you find financial success, joy, and everything you need or want to

live an abundant life!

I close with the words of my former principal who said, "We don't always remember what people say, but we do remember how they make us feel." As our time has now come to an end, I hope I have made you feel loved and empowered to use your money as a tool to achieve your heart's desires. And as always in parting, **"Financial Success is not a gift; it is a Habit!"**

ABOUT THE AUTHOR

Author of Mind Over Money, How to Live Like a Millionaire on Any Budget, Veteran Teacher, Real Estate Investor, & World Traveler, Timolin Langin grew from roots in a small town in Mississippi. There, a generation of relatives with a "mother's wit" for financial success taught her how humble earnings could yield a fiscal life stable enough to support all her dreams, travels, and interests. Her first lessons were given to her by her grandmother, great-grandmother (mother's side), and father. They were good stewards of money who passed on sensible spending habits and wealth building money management practices by example.

Timolin's financial success has been a logical progression. But after watching many smart people struggle with their finances, she realized that her money sense is an uncommon gift. She has decided to share her practical habits for financial success and easy to implement tips that have enabled her to live like a millionaire on her modest teacher's salary. She proves that financial success is less about actual income or specific dollar amount and more about effective money management, passion and purpose, and a zest for living. Whether you make $10,000 per year or $10, 000,000 per year, there are similar philosophies and universal truths needed by all who seek to grow wealth.

If we are faithful with little, we will be faithful with much. More will be given if we address the emotional aspect of our spending and practice money principles that lead to financial success. Timolin lives by these universal truths and believes them essential to growing and maintaining wealth for generations. She places great emphasis on faithfulness to your purpose, not the actual amount of money you have currently. In this book she demonstrates how powerful this concept is in building wealth and helps you take your own steps toward a life well lived in true abundance.

This belief fuels her talks, her blogs, her videos and her website. Timolin is also a contributing author to <u>Stuff Your Face or Face Your</u>

<u>Stuff</u>, a book by TV show "Hoarders" star, Dorothy "the Organizer" Breininger. In that book, Timolin first introduced the importance of Emotional Spending/Overspending as a factor in people's money problems. In her most recent work, she extends her insights into solutions with focus on aligning feelings, thoughts, and actions in relation to money in one's life. She offers ways to increase wealth, decrease debt through strategic spending, increase savings, grow powerful investments, and develop multiple streams of income with creative entrepreneurship.

Timolin currently reveals financial success tips to her clients and audience via her website and You Tube channel. She fervently believes this wealth building message she teaches is universal and wants to share it with the world. Her newest class called "The Creative Dollar" is an organic outgrowth of this book. She closes all of her talks, blogs, and speaking engagements with these words: **Financial Success is not a gift; it is a HABIT!**

NewFitWorldTV.com

Timolin is available for television/radio interviews, public speaking, and other media relations around the world. She also hosts workshops, seminars, and retreats. For more information, visit NewFitWorldTV.com.

DISCLAIMER

This publication is designed to provide accurate and authoritative information in regard to the subject matter covered. It is published with the understanding that the publisher and author are not engaged in rendering legal, accounting, financial, or any professional advice or service. If legal, financial, or professional advice is required, the services of a competent professional person should be sought. Neither the author nor publisher shall be liable for damages arising herein. The fact that an organization or website is referred to in this work as a citation and/or a potential source of further information does not mean that the author or the publisher endorses the information the organization or website may provide or recommendations it may make. Further readers should be aware that internet websites, data, and other references listed in this work may have changed or disappeared between when this work was written and when it is read.

BIBLIOGRAPHY

[1] Henry, Zoe (2016, January 27) *"5 Smart Money Saving Tips from Tony Robbins Financial Adviser"*, **Inc.** www.**inc**.com/**zoe-henry**/tony-robbins-financial-advisor-**tips**-for-entrepreneurs.html

[2] Sanburn, Josh (2012, April 19*) PSYCHOLOGY OF MONEY, Why $50,000 May Be the (New) Happiness Tipping Point* TIME Magazine business.time.com/2012/.../why-50000-**may-be-the-new**-happiness-**tipping-point**.

[3] Sample, Ian (2010, September 6*) "The Price of Happiness"* The Guardianwww.theguardian.com › Science › Psychology

[4] Breininger, Dorothy (2013) *Stuff Your Face or Face Your Stuff* Health Communications, Inc.

[5] Lindstrom, Martin (2015, January) "90 Percent of All Purchasing Decisions are Made Subconsciously" ISPO News mag.ispo.com/.../**90-percent-of-all-purchasing-decisions-are-made-subconsciously**/?

[6] Census. Gov

[7] Kiernan, John (2014, May 27) *"Ask the Experts: How Can We Improve Financial Literacy in the United States?"* www.cardhub.com/edu/**ask-the-experts-financial-literacy**-policy/

[8] Bach, David (2015, July 23) Quoted in Work It, Lynchburg The Information Center for Central Virginia Business The News & Advance www.newsadvance.com/.../**financial-education-needs**...**part-of-our**...The News & Advance

[9] Fottrell, Quenten (2015, June 14) *"10 things billionaires won't tell you"* Market Watch www.marketwatch.com'

REFERENCES

Holy Bible: (1611 Edition) King James Version

Terkeurst, Lysa Proverbs 31 Ministries

Tucker, Stephanie (2010) The *Christian Codependence Workbook*. Huntington Beach, CA: Spirit of Life Recovery Resources

Kuhn, Thomas (1962*) The Structure of Scientific Revolutions* University of Chicago Press Chicago, IL

Lindstrom, Martin (2015, January) *90Percent of All Purchasing Decisions Are Made Subconsciously* ISPO News mag.ispo.com/.../**90-percent-of-all-purchasing-decisions-are-made-subconsciously/** ?

Kahneman, Daniel (2011, October 2) *Thinking, Fast and Slow* Farrar, Straus, and Giroux New York, NY

Wolf, Talia (2014, January 25) *"How Different Colors Are Convincing You to Buy Things"* Business Insider businesswolf.org/how-**different-colors-are-convincing-you-to-buy-things/**

Hill, Napoleon (1928) *Law of Success* Tribeca Books Lindenhurst, NY

Byrnes, Rhonda (2006, November 26) *The Secret* Simon & Schuster, New York, NY

Beyond Words Publishing Hillsboro, OR

Bach, David (2005) *The Automatic Millionaire, A Powerful One-step Plan to Live and Finish Rich* Broadway Books New York, NY

Schlossberg, Mallory (2016, March 10) *The billionaire founder of Ikea has some bizarrely frugal habits* Business Insider www.**businessinsider**.com/ most-**frugal-billionaires**-2013-1

Torre, Pablo S. (2009, March 23) Sports Illustrated Vault www.**si**.com/ vault/2009/03/23/105789480/how-and-why-athletes-**go-broke**

Golden Girl Finance (2013, April 24) *Riches to rags: Why most lottery winners end up broke* GoldenGirlFinance.com https://ca.finance.yahoo. com/.../**riches-rags-why-most-lot**...

Shakespeare, William (1603) *Hamlet*

Hill, Napoleon (1953) *Think and Grow Rich* The Ralston Publishing Cleveland, OH

INDEX

A

Abundance ix, xii, xiii, 1, 4, 6, 9, 17,
   18, 26, 38, 46, 51, 56, 57, 59,
   65, 67, 70, 78, 81, 87, 92, 99,
   100, 102, 105, 107
Action v, xi, xii, xiv, 2, 5, 6, 9, 10, 21,
   26, 31, 32, 36, 38, 42, 44, 47,
   57, 58, 68, 78, 80, 82, 83, 86,
   87, 89, 92, 93, 95, 96, 99, 100,
   101, 102, 103, 105, 108
Advertisers 2, 29, 31, 32, 33, 37, 58, 79
Agrarian Age 39, 41, 42, 47, 51, 78
Alcohol 33, 88, 93
Attraction 49, 75, 99, 100

B

Banks ix, xiii, 3, 15, 16, 41, 42, 43, 44,
   45, 53, 65, 80, 90, 92, 96, 97,
   104
Behavior viii, ix, xi, 1, 4, 5, 6, 9, 10,
   11, 12, 13, 16, 17, 24, 25, 26,
   28, 29, 30, 32, 33, 35, 38, 39,
   45, 55, 57, 58, 60, 61, 78, 79,
   80, 95
Being v, viii, xi, 2, 5, 6, 11, 13, 15, 16,
   17, 18, 19, 25, 26, 30, 33, 35,
   36, 38, 39, 40, 44, 50, 51, 52,
   54, 55, 56, 57, 62, 64, 68, 70,
   72, 73, 74, 78, 83, 91, 96, 100,
   102
Billionaire 16, 65, 105, 110, 112
Born to Do 102
Brain Surgery 5
Budgetary consequences 35

C

Colors 30, 31, 32, 35, 82, 111
Connection xi, xii, xiii, xiv, 5, 6, 14,
   25, 28, 34, 35, 44, 51, 55, 66,
   80, 99
Conscious 1, 4, 9, 10, 11, 12, 18, 25,
   30, 37, 38, 53, 58, 61, 63, 69,
   72, 78, 79, 87, 90, 94, 96
Crave xi, 30
Credit Cards ix, x, 2, 8, 11, 12, 41, 42,
   43, 44, 45, 46, 56, 58, 59, 68,
   69, 70, 74, 80, 88, 94

D

Debt Weight 7, 32, 47, 48, 65, 90
Desperation 22

E

Economics ix, 3, 29, 30, 40, 41, 46, 51,
   69, 104
Emotional Decisions 5
Emotional Overspending v, vi, x, xi,
   xiii, 1, 12, 23, 25, 29, 30, 33, 34,
   35, 36, 37, 54, 59, 70, 88, 91
Emotional Roots viii, x
Emotional Spending xiii, 28, 29, 33,
   108
Emotional Triggers x, 36
Enough xii, xiii, 6, 11, 15, 16, 18, 24,
   26, 34, 35, 43, 56, 58, 67, 70,
   73, 74, 75, 77, 78, 81, 91, 99,
   105, 107

F

Family Influences xiv
Feeling v, viii, x, xi, xii, xiii, xiv, 2, 4, 5,
    9, 10, 11, 12, 13, 14, 17, 18, 19,
    22, 23, 24, 25, 26, 31, 32, 33,
    34, 36, 37, 38, 41, 44, 52, 55,
    56, 63, 66, 67, 77, 79, 81, 85,
    99, 100, 104, 108
Financial Clout 3
Financial community 6, 51
Financial Distress x, xi, xiii, 4, 26, 56,
    63
Financial Farmacy 36
Financial help viii, 34, 50
Financial Journey 6, 26, 27, 54
Financial Literacy 4, 46, 110
Financial savvy 3, 36
Financial security 46
Financial Success ix, xiii, xiv, 4, 10, 12,
    25, 35, 41, 47, 48, 49, 53, 54,
    55, 59, 65, 70, 72, 81, 82, 83,
    85, 86, 99, 102, 104, 106, 107,
    108
Financial Tips 68
Financial World 12, 41
Fruit 36, 47, 48, 57, 101
Fun v, 7, 22, 45, 51, 64, 65, 72, 73, 86,
    90, 95, 96

G

Giving x, xi, xiii, 6, 21, 25, 28, 29, 34,
    36, 58, 71, 85, 86
Good Life 2, 4, 16, 52, 62, 82

H

Habits v, 7, 14, 29, 37, 45, 46, 48, 58,
    61, 70, 74, 80, 81, 86, 92, 93,
    94, 96, 106, 107, 108, 112
Happy vi, 6, 16, 17, 18, 26, 33, 39, 77,
    80, 86, 96
Heuristic knowledge 46, 61, 85, 86

I

Industrial Revolution 43, 50
Information Age 39, 40, 42, 44, 51,
    52, 102

L

Lack x, xii, xiii, 15, 17, 29, 38, 46, 58,
    65, 67, 71, 77, 78, 87
Language 104
Legacy v, xiv, 2, 6, 52, 104, 105
Life of your Dreams 5, 105
Lifetime v, 3, 46, 67, 68, 73, 104
"Little oil" iv, xii, xiii, 1, 3, 58, 65

M

Millionaire i, v, vi, viii, ix, xii, xiii, xiv,
    3, 5, 9, 16, 17, 20, 52, 57, 68,
    82, 101, 102, 105, 107, 111
Mindful 30, 35, 36, 37, 54, 79
Mindless Shopping 3
Mis-connecting 11
Mississippi Delta 2
Money Magnet 20, 83, 96, 99, 100
Money Tool vi, viii, 18, 25, 27, 49, 54,
    66, 70
Money woes 29
More v, vi, ix, x, xi, xii, xiii, xiv, 2, 3, 4,
    7, 9, 12, 14, 15, 16, 17, 18, 19,
    20, 21, 22, 23, 24, 25, 26, 27,
    28, 29, 33, 34, 35, 37, 39, 40,
    41, 42, 43, 44, 46, 47, 49, 50,
    51, 52, 53, 56, 58, 59, 60, 61,
    62, 63, 64, 65, 66, 67, 68, 69,
    70, 71, 72, 74, 75, 76, 77, 78,
    79, 80, 81, 82, 83, 85, 86, 87,
    89, 90, 91, 92, 94, 99, 100, 105,
    107, 108

N

Network 6, 7, 40, 94
Neuro-marketing 29, 31, 33, 36
New Fit World TV 4, 45, 75, 82, 89
NewFitWorldTv.com 4, 6, 37, 51, 86,
    89, 94, 108
Now v, vi, ix, xi, xiii, xiv, 2, 3, 4, 5, 6,
    7, 8, 9, 11, 12, 15, 18, 19, 20,
    21, 22, 26, 32, 36, 39, 40, 42,
    45, 47, 49, 51, 55, 56, 57, 58,
    62, 65, 66, 68, 69, 70, 72, 73,
    74, 82, 87, 90, 91, 92, 94, 96,
    99, 102, 105, 106

O

One-person Corporation 102

P

Pain xi, 2, 4, 24, 32, 33, 35, 36, 51,
    63, 77
Paradigm Shifts xiii, xiv, 9, 10, 13, 16,
    18, 21, 26, 27, 28, 35, 39, 41,
    43, 47, 53, 54, 55, 59, 74, 102
Popular 34, 43, 55, 64, 67
Pressure x, 15, 17, 20, 67, 73
"Procrasteneur" 51
Purpose viii, 4, 5, 6, 24, 27, 35, 38, 46,
    49, 54, 61, 70, 73, 77, 86, 100,
    104, 105, 106, 107
Purposeful Dollar 14, 70

R

Relationship with money 37
Research 4, 11, 16, 29, 30, 31, 34, 36,
    38, 58, 62, 64, 77, 85, 100, 102
Resource v, viii, xii, 1, 6, 26, 37, 38, 41,
    46, 49, 51, 52, 53, 61, 67, 70,
    81, 90, 99, 100, 101, 105, 111
Results x, xi, 9, 10, 11, 12, 15, 20, 21,
    22, 23, 25, 26, 29, 33, 35, 44,
    46, 47, 48, 49, 57, 63, 64, 65,
    74, 79, 92, 94, 97, 105
Retail therapy 31, 33, 34, 35

S

Saving challenges 51, 86, 92, 94
Scientific 9, 10, 18, 22, 23, 39, 53, 85,
    111
Small income 1, 67
Solutions 21, 37, 79, 108
Sports Illustrated 63, 112
State of mind ix, 1, 5, 6, 11, 16, 17, 38,
    39, 55, 57, 62, 63, 75
Stewardship ix, 73, 75
Strategic Application of Knowledge 22
Strategic Spending 14, 36, 42, 65, 72,
    100, 108

T

"Teacherpreneur" 101, 102
Technology 11, 40, 45, 51, 53, 54
Thinking x, xii, xiii, xiv, 2, 4, 5, 6, 9,
    10, 12, 13, 17, 18, 19, 20, 22,
    23, 24, 25, 26, 29, 30, 33, 35,
    36, 38, 39, 55, 56, 57, 58, 69,
    73, 74, 76, 77, 78, 82, 90, 99,
    101, 102, 111
Transform ix, xiii, 9, 15, 52, 53
Transformation vi, xii, xiv, 1, 10, 12,
    30, 39, 40, 43, 51, 53, 80, 82,
    83, 87, 88, 89, 91, 99, 101, 103
Twelve 53, 55, 56, 57, 80, 87
Twenty one 71

U

Unconscious x, 10, 11, 14, 15, 32, 78,
    79, 91

V

Vision 18, 19, 49, 50, 51, 60, 61, 65,
    70, 81, 89, 100, 102, 103

W

Wait strategy 69
Wealth v, xi, xiii, xiv, 1, 5, 6, 9, 10, 18,
    19, 20, 25, 26, 37, 38, 39, 41,
    45, 47, 48, 50, 51, 53, 57, 58,

59, 61, 62, 65, 66, 67, 68, 69,
70, 75, 78, 84, 85, 86, 94, 99,
100, 101, 104, 105, 107, 108
Wealth building xi, xiii, xiv, 6, 41, 53,
58, 65, 66, 67, 68, 70, 75, 84,
85, 86, 104, 107, 108
Worldwide 45, 51, 104
Written plan 69

Printed in the United States
By Bookmasters